OL' BOYD

OL' BOYD

JUST PLAIN GOOD READIN'
Book I

A collection of columns written
by Bill Boyd
Columnist for the Macon Telegraph and News

Compiled and edited
by Bill Boyd
and Barbara Stinson

with a Foreword
by Billy Watson

Printed in the United States of America.
Published by Bill Boyd
Macon Telegraph and News
P. O. Box 4167
Macon, Georgia 31213

Contents

Dedication

For

*All of the "young" folks
who can say they are 80 . . .
and smile about it.*

Foreword

It was a sight I will not soon forget. The floor of the huge Macon Coliseum was almost filled with elderly people who had come to Bill Boyd's first 80-and-Over Birthday Party. And there among them, doing his best to comply with all the requests for autographs, was Ol' Boyd.

Most newspaper people nowadays, in an era of strong anti-press sentiment, wonder if they ought to duck when a stranger approaches. Bill gets ready for fan worship.

The popularity of this ex-Marine who didn't begin column-writing until he approached midlife is truly remarkable. It is due in part to the sort of guy he is and in part to the sorts of columns he writes, and the two, of course, are closely interrelated.

Those who know Bill only through his five-a-week columns in the Macon Telegraph and News probably would agree with my favorite description of him as a self-described redneck who keeps things interesting with occasional lapses into fits of liberalism.

His columns reflect the basic values he learned during a tough growing-up period as one of 18 children of a sharecropper in Oklahoma and Texas. His writings preach the virtues of honesty, hard work, patriotism, self-reliance, decency and loyalty. His tone ranges from blazing anger to tender compassion. His subjects are mostly decent, law-abiding folks who otherwise get their names in the paper only when they are born, get married and die.

Perhaps what distinguishes Bill from a lot of other writers is the relationships he develops with the people he writes about. His is not the hit-and-run interview approach. The subject of a Boyd column often becomes a life-long Boyd friend or admirer, or both.

After he did a prize-winning series of stories about Mennonites in nearby Macon County, several of them spent a long day helping Bill, Marvalene and son Joe move into their first home. He carried on a shameless and blatant three-year "love affair" with "Miss Cleo" (she's in the book), the adopted "grandmother" of the Atlanta Braves, before she died in April 1982 at age 101. After an initial column about a three-year-old victim of leukemia, Bill stayed close to the family until the boy's tragic death two years later, calling the mother at 2 a.m. in a Memphis hotel room because there was no phone in the child's hospital room. Bill still carries a scar on his leg—the result of a chainsaw injury sustained while helping a correspondent's husband cut firewood. He constantly drops into nursing homes, just to chat with the elderly residents, many of whom have been mentioned in his articles.

His is a journalism of the heart, and it mostly came naturally. Bill's only formal journalistic training was in high school. He worked parttime for several papers during 20 years in the Marines, then joined The Macon Telegraph as a roving photo journalist in 1973. His aggressiveness and gregariousness led to the development of numerous sources and a flood of photos and stories, and soon he was state news editor. In December 1977 he began writing a column for the Saturday paper. He expanded it to twice a week, adding Sundays, in late 1980, and as awards began to come in and the fan mail grew, he went to fulltime column-writing in early 1982.

During 1984 he will make more than 100 speeches, receive from 1,500 to 2,500 cards and letters (some 500 will relate to his 80-and-Over Club), and answer upwards of 3,500 phone calls at the office and at home.

Yet he will find time to do countless favors for his friends, because he is a person who genuinely likes his fellow human beings. That is obvious to anyone who reads his columns regularly, and I suspect that that, more than any other single thing, explains his success.

Billy Watson
General Manager
The Macon Telegraph and News

FOLKS
WHO LOVED ME

If there's any combination of people and places that could love a poor boy from Oklahoma, I suppose it would have to be a taxi-driving stepdaddy from Arkansas, a clothes-scrubbing mama from Ohio, a sharecropper's daughter from Florida, an adopted son who paid his childhood debts with candy-coated kisses, and a town named Macon, Georgia. Lucky me, I found them all.

A Touch
of Class

The Oklahoma family scattered after the father died. The older children kissed their mother goodbye and went to live with relatives while she re-organized her life.

Another man brought the family back together, a man from Arkansas.

An old heap of a taxi was his only transportation. He drove it 12 to 15 hours a day for the rich man who could afford many taxis.

Hacking wasn't much of a living in the late 1940s. A little black change purse with a single snap at the top was a good enough bank. The Arkansas man managed to stay close to even with the world.

The driver's license was his ticket, like a college degree to other folks. With it he could "always make a living."

Along came the young widow with four boys, the youngest just 2; the oldest 13. Romance blossomed under a sign that flashed "Taxi Here."

The Arkansas man and the widow sat on a worn bench and talked. Little boys played at their feet. Bigger boys rambled around the Oklahoma town.

A year passed before he popped the question. "Let's get married in Fort Smith (Arkansas)," he said.

"Never been to Fort Smith," she replied. In fact, the widow had never ridden 100 miles in a car at one time. Her dead husband had been a share-cropper, with only two horses and a wagon.

The widow scrubbed up her kids. The Arkansas man rented his taxi for the day. They headed for Fort Smith.

People in every little town tried to flag the old taxi down.

But they said their vows in Fort Smith, and whitewash was used to letter "Just Married" on the taxi for the return trip.

People in the small towns smiled and waved to them on the trip home.

Daddy Philpot brought stability and laughter back to the family. Good days returned for the widow and the four boys.

The Arkansas man came to want a car for his family. He took a second job as constable of the Oklahoma town, serving papers on people who didn't pay their bills.

But there never seemed to be enough money to raise four boys. Still, dimes once a week paid for the movies—Roy Rogers, Gene Autry, The Sunset Kid. He even gave them an extra nickel for popcorn, although Daddy Philpot called movies "foolishness."

He was good for the economy, always a little in debt, never hoarding money.

Times were hard, but he refused to let them get desperate. Some of his sayings didn't make much sense to teen-age boys:

"Always be honest. Money can take honesty away, but it can't buy it back."

"Don't trust a man who talks too much. A man can talk just so long, and keep telling the truth."

"Be careful of a man who borrows money. He's already in money trouble."

His sayings made more sense to the boys when they grew up.

Twelve years passed, the older boys moved away. But Daddy Philpot got sick, and they gathered at his bedside. Their visit was like a tonic; he went home.

Another week passed. Death came to the Arkansas man.

This time the boys came to bury him, pooling their money for a good funeral. A final touch of class—something he could never afford.

More years passed. The widow married again and moved away. The children seldom returned to the grave in Oklahoma.

Years dimmed memories. A son checked a logbook at the cemetery to locate Daddy Philpot's grave. Beside his name a notation: $15 due.

Yes, said the caretaker, but this is an old debt, almost 20 years old.

I pulled $15 from my pocket. Daddy Philpot was finally even with the world.

Learning
at Home

She didn't look like a schoolteacher. Her hair was never pinned up quite as neatly as a schoolmarm's. But then, schoolmarms seldom went straight from a washboard to a blackboard.

She didn't have the formal education of most schoolteachers. Hers ended in the 11th grade.

The books she used weren't the latest editions. Primers were old and the covers faded. Workbooks were tattered and pages were missing.

But in a covered wagon traveling the arid roads of Oklahoma and Texas, the plump, pleasant woman found time to teach her offspring.

Her handwriting was as straight and perfect as examples posted above blackboards in classrooms.

Her children tried to write as straight and perfect as she did. But their efforts often looked like notes scribbled in a moving wagon.

She was a good reader. She honed that skill reading old western romance magazines she borrowed from others.

And she taught her kids to read from primers and old newspapers. Because of the times, Adolph Hitler was mentioned as often as George Washington, and Pearl Harbor seemed closer than El Paso.

Her arithmetic was accurate. She learned it by figuring her grocery money over and over.

And Lord knows, that lady could spell. She was the second best speller in all of Ohio in the eighth grade.

She'd look at a kid who was supposed to be in the third grade and say, "Spell incomprehensibility." If the kid stuttered, he'd offer a silent prayer he wasn't being taught by whoever beat his mama in the state spelling bee.

The woman taught her brood in the covered wagon, around a campfire, and by kerosene lamps in old houses when the father could find work on a farm.

While her husband, an older, stoop-shouldered man, worked in sun-baked fields with a mule and plow, she taught patience, reverence and independence right along with reading, writing and arithmetic.

She kept a small, faded American flag from a long-ago parade in Tulsa. She'd hold the flag in one hand while the kids put a hand over their hearts and recited the Pledge of Allegiance.

The family settled for a while in west Texas, where the father rode a horse and looked after scraggly long-horn cattle. They lived in an adobe shack that was 40 miles or more from the nearest school. And the mother kept teaching.

Before the war ended, the family moved to eastern Oklahoma. The trip took months, but the mother never stopped teaching.

The mother expressed thanks that her children could finally attend "a real school." And for the first time, a 9-year-old boy sat in a classroom.

How good was the mother's home teaching?

The boy was tested and placed in the fourth grade. He went on to get a high school education, and even attended college for a few months. Her teachings in reading, writing and arithmetic—along with spelling, Lord knows—eventually led to a career in writing.

Maybe you've guessed by now that this woman—the spelling champ, the disciplinarian, the patriotic soul with a little American flag in one hand—was my mother.

And maybe you also know the General Assembly will begin debating today over a parent's right to teach his or her children at home.

If Momma were to express an opinion about this—and she's certainly paid her dues—I think she would say:

• She wouldn't have taught her own children if she could have put them in a good school.

• Parents who teach at home ought to be as qualified as teachers in regular schools.

• Parents ought not to gamble with their children's education, not for the sake of egos, not for religious beliefs, not for any reason.

In other words, if you can't spell "incomprehensibility," you may have your children suffering from it.

Our Strange Little Habits

It's strange how two people who live together a lot of years pick up strange little habits.

Some of these mutual but unspoken agreements may seem silly to anyone but the two sharing the habit.

For instance, I once worked with a guy who said his sandwich just wouldn't taste right unless his wife took a bite out of it before she wrapped it. Sure enough, every time he unwrapped a sandwich from his lunch pail, a big bite was missing.

I thought he was crazy until Marvalene started our habit of sharing a soft drink.

As I recall, it started soon after we began dating. We knew each other just well enough by then to talk about some of the important things in life—like making a living.

We'd just finished a conversation about money and stopped at a little hamburger joint for lunch. That's when Marvalene decided to economize. She ordered two hamburgers and just one Coke.

"Where's the other Coke?" I asked.

She began pouring the Coke into two little cups. "One is enough."

"Why didn't you get two?"

"Well, you said money is tight. So I just bought one."

"Don't be silly."

"I'm not. I'm just saving money."

"A lousy quarter."

"But a quarter."

"You're nuts."

"Uh-huh."

We each drank half a Coke and enjoyed it.

The next time we ate together in a restaurant, we bought just one soft drink. The guy behind the counter looked from one to the other and asked, "Just one Coke?"

I said, "Just one," and he shook his head as he went to fill our order.

We decided to really pick on the guy. Next time we went there, we ordered just one order of french fries and split it, too. More head shaking.

I wanted to order a slice of apple pie and ask for two forks, but Marvalene said we'd already worried the guy enough.

It never did get easy to convince waiters and waitresses that we wanted just one soft drink. And there were occasions when we shared other drinks, too.

For instance, we once ordered one glass of wine in a posh restaurant and passed it back and forth. Those folks are probably still talking about the couple who ate filet mignon but were too cheap to buy two glasses of wine.

There were fewer questions after Joe adopted us. Folks behind the counter could forgive us for ordering just two Cokes when Joe was a little tyke.

But now he's taller than his mother and the questions have resumed anytime we order two drinks for the three of us.

Just a few days ago, we stopped at a fast-food restaurant, and a young woman took our orders.

We ordered three large sandwiches and two drinks. She couldn't wait to prove to me that she could count all the way to three.

"Just two drinks?"

"Yes."

She looked from me to Marvalene to Joe. I guess she was trying to figure out who was going to choke on a sandwich.

"Just *two* drinks?" she asked again.

I gave her my best smile and said, "*Exactly* two."

"But doesn't he want something to drink?" she asked, gesturing toward Joe.

"He has a drink."

"Oh."

I guess the questions will never stop. Just as long as we try to share a Coke, someone will want to sell us two.

Say, I wonder how much money we've saved in the last 17 years? If we keep sharing for the next eight years. . . .

Twenty-five years of sharing Cokes? Maybe we can afford that cruise Marvalene keeps talking about. A man ought to do something special at a time like that.

She's Still 'Super'

She is not a superwoman. She never could leap tall buildings in a single bound. But she got caught up in the "superwoman syndrome."

Let me tell you about it. She's been a mother for 10 1/2 years, a wife for 17. She's been a breadwinner and a housekeeper virtually all of her life.

But she isn't superwoman. It took a near-tragedy to discover that.

She developed her steely fiber in the fertile farm fields of South Florida. Her father was a sharecropper, and she spent endless hours working under a hot sun in vegetable fields.

In her teen years, she worked harder than many adult women ever have to.

By the time she finished high school, she was a licensed beautician. And when she attended night college classes, she worked fulltime.

And by the time she was 21, she'd carved a comfortable niche for herself.

When she married, she never thought of quitting. Two incomes were better than one, she said many times. And she kept working at a most tiring kind of job.

Walking around a beautician's chair all day isn't a job for wimps or weaklings. It'll make even a superwoman want to sit down.

She fell headlong into the "superwoman syndrome" in her mid-30s.

She was a mother. She had one child, and she watched over him as only a mother can watch over her only child. And as soon as he was old enough for school, she returned to full-time employment.

Her responsibilities had increased gradually—a husband, then a son, returning to a full-time job, and finally, extensive volunteer work.

Yes, when others saw her dedication for getting the job done, she was "drafted" onto the board of directors of the Little League, and the PTA people wanted her, too. They praised her efforts. She was chosen "Parent of the Year" by the PTA.

At one time, she was both president of the PTA and vice president of the Little League.

Then she collapsed. It happened the morning after the PTA gave her a "Parent of the Year" plaque. She was working hard at her job when she keeled over.

The next few days were scary for the husband and son. Tests and waiting. Wringing hands and swallowing lumps. The doctor finally analyzed the condition: exhaustion and high blood pressure. A deadly combination, he said.

The woman went home to the comfortable house she cared for and helped pay for. And she rested.

The family wised up—husband, son and would-be superwoman. The husband and son did all sorts of house chores—picking up after themselves, washing clothes, bringing in meals.

The would-be superwoman made a promise. She'd find an hour out of every day that would be hers, even if it was 15 minutes here and 15 minutes there. Or sometimes she'd get a full hour while her husband took their son somewhere . . . anywhere.

But life had to slow down.

The woman didn't take on as many outside projects. The family took long weekends camping and traveling together. And when they went, the woman didn't cook or worry about other chores. She relaxed.

They ate out more often.

A maid—a luxury a sharecropper's daughter never considered—was hired to do some of the heavier housework.

The woman made her comeback. And of course, she went back to work.

But life never will be the same. Not since we—son Joe and I—found out that our Marvalene is not superwoman.

It's taken 2 1/2 years to really win a round. And another round is always there to be won again. Still, we're very happy we didn't have to pay a higher price to learn.

And we wanted to share this story with others who think they know a superwoman.

Home Is
Where . . .

OKMULGEE, Okla.—Someone once said you can't go home again. But people keep fooling themselves.

I did. I went home because I wanted son Joe, 12, to see where his old man grew up.

And what does a man show his son after a 30-year absence? I made a list.

First, the Baptist Church. Every man ought to show his son where he learned about Jesus.

Second, the pool hall. That's a different kind of learning, but it wasn't all bad.

And Joe ought to see the places I lived, the school where I learned, the theaters where I watched Gene Autry and Sunset Carson, the bakery where I could buy a loaf of piping-hot bread out the back door for a dime after church on Sunday night.

Lots of places needed a second look.

The Creek Indian Council House sits on the square here. I parked and looked at it.

"Looks the same," I said. But it obviously wasn't.

Late on a hot August afternoon, as many as 200 people used to gather on the square, sit on green benches and fan away at the heat.

Not now. Air conditioning killed a tradition. Three elderly men sat on green benches. Two kids romped nearby. That's all.

It's just as well that 200 people didn't show up. They couldn't all sit on just six benches that remain.

But the theaters. They're still right over . . . . I looked around.

The Inca is gone. Appliances glared at me from where huge posters of Roy Rogers and Trigger once hung.

The Yale is gone, too. A dress shop took over. Women try on fashions where I once cooled my heels in air-conditioned comfort, sipped nickel Cokes, and rooted for Red Ryder and Little Beaver.

The Orpheum. It's still there. But we never went there until we started liking girls. Girls. I thought back.

The first date there? Uh, her name was, uh . . . well, it isn't important.

I pointed Joe toward a building I especially wanted him to see—the up-stairs apartment where we lived when Momma met Daddy Philpot, the step-daddy who reared me from 11 to 18. It's easy to find because there's a beer joint under it with a jukebox that plays Hank Williams songs late into the night. . . .

Gone, too. Another magic poof from the elapse of 30 years. A parking lot and one of those little buildings for drive-through banking is the modern version of a beer joint with a walk-up apartment over it.

The office where I joined the Marines? It moved out of the post office. I didn't bother to ask where.

The first Baptist Church? Another parking lot. Oh, there's a big brick church by the same name right across the street, but I'd like to know if Jesus smiled when they tore down the building where I used to talk to him.

The People's Bakery where I bought piping-hot bread after church? It's still there. The old sign still hangs diagonally on the corner. But sorry, no hot bread after church, a clerk said. Only doughnuts and sweet rolls come out of the back now. Bread is trucked in from Tulsa.

I steered Joe toward Sixth Street. I wanted him to see the pool hall. On the way, I told him about the rule my parents set down: The sign may say you can shoot pool at 16, but you won't go there until you're 18 and on your own. It wasn't easy to learn to shoot pool with one eye on the door and the other on the cueball.

Gone.

A woman said it burned to the ground three years ago. My Momma used to hope it would happen. She was afraid it would see more of me than the First Baptist Church.

"Hey, Dad, how about a game of Pac-Man?" Joe said, breaking into my memories.

He'd spied a game room of another kind a few doors from where the pool hall once stood.

"Pac-Man?" I said. "Sure, why not? We could use a little relaxation before we start home. . . ."

Home. I looked down Sixth Street toward Macon . . . toward home.

My Special Christmas Card

A special Christmas present arrived a few days ago in the home of a young couple I know. 'Twas a baby girl.

But it took five years for them to get the baby. They did it the hard way—adoption.

Marvalene said it would make a great Christmas column. I agreed. The young couple didn't.

Seems they didn't want their names or pictures in the paper for fear of someone figuring out exactly where the baby came from.

The young couple said I should understand since the Boyds had gone through the same sort of thing.

Understand? Sure, I understand. It's shaky when that kid first moves into the home. . . .

Ten years ago.

Has it really been so long?

Marvalene and I were married six years, and we'd certainly tried the method nature provided. But we'd struck out in the baby department.

We flatly refused to go through fertility tests to find out whose "fault" it was. Besides, when we'd heard all that, where would we be?

We decided to try adoption.

First, we talked to a private adoption agency. We learned the agency needed six months or more to conduct a "home study." And the waiting list was maybe three years long. Since the Marine Corps was telling us where we'd live next, it was unlikely we'd be there long enough to bingo.

Besides, we didn't seem to impress the agency. We weren't rich, and those people always appeared more concerned with collecting money than placing children.

So we pulled out.

Next, we tried the welfare department. Things worked better and faster. They asked us if we'd take a child "who isn't perfect." We said, heck, yes. We couldn't remember ever knowing a perfect child anyhow.

Within a year—on Dec. 26, 1972—the caseworker told us we were accepted. We could expect a child in a month. That was just about the best Christmas gift that ever arrived on Dec. 26. And almost a month later, she called to say she wanted us to meet a 20-month-old boy.

I was captivated by him. He was a little chubby, maybe a little scared.

On a Monday, we took him out to the apartment for a "visit." He got passed around like a loaf of bread, but he didn't seem to mind.

The second visit came two days later, and he spent all day with us. When the welfare people tried to take him back, he hung on my neck and cried. He gave them a tough time, and I wanted to take his side.

On Friday of that week, he moved in with us. And it was shaky.

At first, we just tried to keep him happy. The first time he cried, I did, too. After that, I learned a little bit about why babies cry—hunger, wet diapers, sleepiness. Marvalene said none of the reasons was serious enough to make a grown man cry. So I quit.

I still recall getting up in the middle of the night and watching him sleeping in his bunk bed. I had to do that when I woke up and wondered if it was all a dream. Sometimes, his momma was already there, staring contentedly at him.

We worried someone would come and try to claim him. But that fear slipped away amidst baby kisses, Christmases together, a tonsillectomy, the first day of school, a Little League championship, vacations. . . .

And the kid who wasn't perfect?

He's 11-1/2 and going on 20 this Christmas. He's as tall as his mother.

Less than perfect? Well, he had a minor speech impairment. But it disappeared so quickly under the coaching of a speech therapist we nicknamed him "motor mouth."

Less than perfect? A doctor recently found a bone in his foot that isn't growing perfectly, and he may face an operation someday that's every bit as serious as removing a hang-nail.

On his last report card, the kid brought home four A's and one B. Hmmm. Maybe that's what the welfare worker meant when she said he was less than perfect. . . .

Yeah, it sure is shaky when a new kid moves in. But I wanted to offer this story in lieu of Christmas cards since the *Macon Telegraph and News* declines to pay the postage on 85,233 Christmas cards.

Merry Christmas from Marvalene, Joe and Ol' Boyd.

JOE,
THE KID
WHO REARED ME

Mama used to say, "When you grow up, you'll learn that I was just trying to do the right thing for you." But she never said I'd learn that lesson from a kid.

Those Were
Good Old Days?

Son Joe showed me his fifth-grade assignment: Ask your parents about changes in the way they live since they were children, and write about it.

Joe grinned and said, "I'll bet you this is different, getting interviewed instead of the other way around."

It was.

I hadn't looked back 38 years and talked about it since. . . . Lord, how long had it been?

The year was 1944 . . . I remember a big house. Make that a big, cold house. It was heated by a pot-bellied stove in the living room and a four-"burner" cookstove in the kitchen. It was air-conditioned by fickle breezes that occasionally stirred the Oklahoma plains.

It was a two-story house. But it was old and dilapidated, and the back stairs had crumbled years ago. A 9-year-old had nightmares about yanking open the nailed-up door and falling, falling. . . .

I broke off the stare through wide, glassy patio doors in our North Macon home and watched Joe scribble his homework. . . .

I remember a well beside the big house. We'd draw water with a galvanized bucket and pour it into dishpans, pails or washtubs to carry it inside.

If there was the slightest hint of dust on the top of the water, we had to do it again. "I don't cook with dirty water," Momma would say. "I don't wash dishes in dirty water. I don't even wash my feet in dirty water."

But when the spring rains turned the water muddy, it didn't mean we got out of taking baths regularly in a big washtub. . . .

Joe was writing a new paragraph about drawing water from a well. He looked up and sort of squinted, maybe looking for a hint of exaggeration. . . .

Blue Monday. Know why they call it that? Momma didn't have a washing machine until some years later. She washed clothes on a scrub board that was partially submerged in what we called a "No. 2 washtub."

In nice weather, she lined a dozen clotheslines with our humble gar-ments. And in foul weather, she'd improvise lines inside near the stove so we'd have decent-looking clothes for school the next day. . . .

Joe turned in his chair. He could see the washer and dryer in the little room off the kitchen, those shiny efficient machines of the 1980s. . . .

Dad was always in the field—urging Old Red along, plowing another furrow between rows of corn that were just popping out of the soil. Dad never owned a tractor, probably couldn't have driven one if he'd had it. Be-sides, he said many a time that a man can't cuss a tractor and be under-stood. Old Red understood Dad's harsh commands and occasional wrath. . . .

Joe's writing turned to plowing with a mule. . . .

And Dad never owned a car, didn't even like to ride in them. He'd tell you flat-out that anyplace worth going to was worth going to in a wagon. Not a buggy, mind you, but a wagon. That was luxury enough to an old man who spent most of his life walking at the south end of a mule from first light 'til sunset to make a poor man's dollar. . . .

Joe's pencil was scratching steadily at the lined notebook paper. . . .

And the plumbing. . . . We didn't have indoor plumbing of our own until after Dad died and we moved away from that sharecropper's farm.

I remember Momma used to tell us to use the bathroom before we left school or church on rainy days. You see, the roof leaked on that old out-house with the door that always squeaked. . . .

I waited a moment while Joe finished. Then he looked up at me and asked, "Why do people keep calling those 'the good old days?' "

I shrugged and said, "Beats me, son."

The sun was setting through the patio doors. I heard the air-conditioner kick on. Joe slapped the books shut and left me with my thoughts. . . .

Catcher's
Cup Episode

The baseball season starts tonight. Yes, I know the Atlanta Braves have been playing for a month. And the Macon Redbirds have been chirping for a couple of weeks.

But I'm talking about *real* baseball—Little League—where kids sometime need coaching on more than just how to field a hot grounder.

I'm thankful son Joe won't be catching this season. One opening night at catcher was enough.

You see, a mighty big decision for a Little Leaguer is what position he wants to play. Naturally, every kid wants to pitch and hit home runs. They dream of doing those things in the Little League World Series.

So Joe didn't really want to be a catcher that season a couple of years ago. He even said so.

But he's a strong kid with a good throwing arm, and in the minor league, they need strong arms behind the plate.

Joe practiced hard and didn't complain. And his parents did their part. We took Joe to every practice, and when he wasn't at the field, I'd throw "fly balls" for him in the front yard.

By opening day, we had a pretty good catcher in the family. And naturally, I made a Scout's-honor promise that I'd be there for the opening game.

It didn't turn out that way. Does it ever? How many times have daddies missed important games?

An unusual sequence of events led up to what is known around our house as "The Catcher's Cup Episode."

I know now that I should have checked with him—just in case he needed some fatherly advice.

He did.

For anyone who doesn't know what a catcher's cup is, let me explain it's a triangular shaped plastic cup that keeps little boys—and grown men—from howling if a foul tip hits the wrong section of the male anatomy.

The first time Joe tried to put on a catcher's cup, Daddy was chasing a red-hot story in another town. By the time I reached the ball field, the game was in the fourth inning.

We were winning, but Joe was chasing passed balls like a ruptured duck. When he batted, he waddled to first base like a sick penguin. I even hollered one time, "Joe, you aren't hustling, son." He gave me an icy stare that said to shut up.

I wondered if a foul tip had hit him where the catcher's cup ought to be.

After the game, he limped toward me, looking like he'd played 20 innings. He told his momma that he wanted to ride home with me.

Once alone, he started telling Daddy all about it.

"Daddy?"

"Yes, son."

"I don't want to be a catcher."

"Whatsa matter, too hot in all that equipment?"

"No."

"You got hit by a foul tip?"

"No. It's the catcher's cup."

"What's wrong with it?"

"It doesn't fit me right. It must have been made for someone else."

"That bad, huh?"

"Yes, can I take it off now?"

"Sure."

He reached into the top of his pants and pulled it out. Only one point of the cup showed as it came into view. So that was what was wrong. He was wearing the darn thing upside down. With the wide side down, it had rubbed him raw on the inside of his thighs.

"Who told you how to wear that thing?"

"Momma."

"Well, she doesn't know. . . . "

"Wait a minute," said my 9-year-old son. "Where were you when I needed you?"

I started trying to explain about the red-hot story, but you know how Little Leaguers are. Catcher's cups are more important than any old news story.

Like I said, I'm glad Joe isn't catching this year. We couldn't stand it if this story ever got out.

Those Little
White Lies

All right, folks, it's time for a tough question most parents would probably rather not answer. But here it is anyhow: Do you ever lie to your kid?

Think hard, now. When we're on the subject of lying—even little white lies—is certainly no time to slip up and, uh, tell another.

Just the other morning, son Joe answered something by saying, "Are you sure?"

I said, "Hey, kid, did your old man ever lie to you?"

I should have bit my tongue off. He looked me straight in the eye and just nodded.

"Naw, I didn't," I said, sounding as offended as possible.

Joe just kept nodding.

"All right, *when* did I lie to you? And be exact. No beating around the bush."

Joe will be a teen-ager in May, and he's getting to that thoughtful stage. So he isn't in a hurry to say the first thing that comes to mind, especially when someone is trying to wiggle out of a corner.

"Well, the first one was maybe . . . gee, I don't know how many years ago. I remember I was pretty small."

"All right, *what* did I lie about?"

I saw a little color creep into his cheeks as he mumbled, "About where babies come from."

"Did I say they were found in a cabbage patch?"

He began shaking his head.

"Not the story about the cabbage patch? Then what did I say?"

He stuck his chin way out and made a flapping motion with his arms.

"The stork?"

He nodded.

"Well, hey. That's an explanation lots of parents give. . . ."

"But it isn't so? Right?"

He had me there.

"Just one lie in all of these years? That isn't too bad. . . ."

"What about the bricks under the Christmas tree?"

I searched a failing memory.

"When was that?"

"Several years ago."

"Bricks? I said there were bricks under the Christmas tree?"

"Yes, sir, you sure did."

"And what was in that box?"

"The ratchet set you gave me to work on my bike."

"Say, a ratchet set is a pretty nice present. . . ."

"But it wasn't bricks."

"Oh, yeah . . . Well, I mean, two little white lies in all these years. . . ."

"And what about the present under the tree this year? You know, the cowboy hat?"

I remembered that box. Maybe my memory isn't so bad after all.

"Sure, I remember what was in that box. The Michael Jackson record."

"Yes, and not a cowboy hat."

"No, but it was a nice present. It had his picture on both sides. And it was something you really wanted. And it was. . . ."

"But it *wasn't* a cowboy hat."

"OK, OK, three little old white lies in all of these years. That isn't so bad. I'll bet you've told me a few."

This time, he looked offended. He did that because we've had a deal since he was old enough to talk. Joe *never* lies to me. Period. In return . . . well, maybe I shouldn't have told even those little white lies.

"Just tell me when I lied," he said.

"Well, there was that time you were playing with a cigarette lighter and you said you didn't. . . ."

"And you let me worry all night and waited for me to 'fess up the next day. I laid awake all night. I'd rather take a licking than lay awake all night."

The kid gave me a hard look and said, "What else?"

"Well, there was . . . hmmmm. . . ."

"Yes, Dad?"

"Uh, yes, well . . . There was the time that, uh. . . ."

"The score is 3-1, Dad."

"Uh-huh. Well, one thing you've gotta say for your old man. He did a pretty good job of bringing you up, didn't he?"

"How do you always find a way to turn things your way?"

"Just part of being a daddy."

'He's 13
Only Once'

I've made up my mind. I'm just not giving in to some of the silly ideas my son comes up with.

Sure, he's going to be 13 in a couple of months, and you know how teen-agers can be. They'll scheme endlessly to outmaneuver adults. But I'm keeping a tight rein, folks.

Watch this. He wants me to go shopping at the mall. Says he needs some new dress clothes. And after all, it was *my* idea that he go to classes to learn proper manners and etiquette, and then attend some of these uptown dinners and other fancy shindigs with his mama and me.

All we're going to do is buy some new clothes. Dress clothes. None of that modish mess that some parents get stuck with. So y'all come along and see how a really smart daddy operates.

First, watch how I guide him straight into a department store. I won't even bother to remind him that if the clothes there are good enough for me, they're good enough for him. That kind of talk will get a teen's back up every time.

I just guide him a little. You know, park at that end of the mall so we enter through the department store.

You can see I did the right thing. He likes the slacks on the far rack. He didn't stop at the same rack I did, but those back there are OK.

Let him try them on. When he emerges from the dressing room, I tell him how nice the slacks look on him. Psychology, folks. A little praise works wonders.

Now that we've selected a pair of dress slacks that I'd be proud to own, let him pick a shirt to go with the slacks. Sure, let him do the choosing.

Sorry, son, that T-shirt with the Japanese writing won't do. In fancy places, you have to wear a shirt with a collar.

Yes, that's nice, the striped one with the short sleeves. (Thank God he didn't go after a muscle shirt.)

Can we look around? Sure, son, just tell the lady to hold those clothes until we get back.

Down the mall we go, peeking into the various shops. I guide him toward a store with more everyday clothes. Well, the jeans are a little modish, but what the heck, the kid isn't looking for jeans.

Say you like that shirt better than the one at the department store, son? Well, OK, but let's look around.

Notice how I guided him out of that shop, folks?

The next place surely sells the wildest clothes of all. But don't worry, I can handle it.

Parachute pants? Is that what he said? Never heard of them.

But I look with him. Why not? Let the kid get it out of his system.

For those who never heard of parachute pants, they're made out of the same silky material as parachutes. They have about 12 yards of zippers that, when unzipped, reveal silk of a different color.

Take my word for it, no one will ever get run over while wearing parachute pants.

He likes that slick black pair. But look at the price tag, I tell him. You can get those nice slacks in the department store and have $5 left for a movie.

He nods agreement. Good kid. I reared him right.

To get him out of there, we go on to a restaurant for dinner. Still, he lobbies. They're the "in" thing, he says. Yes, they're expensive, but he promises to take good care of them. He won't even slide into second base, he says.

I send him on a useless errand so I can talk to his mother.

"What do you think?"

"No, what do you think?"

I shrug. "He's 13 only once."

"And he'll take care of them. He did all right with that designer jacket."

"But he can't wear them to dinners, etiquette classes, that sort of thing."

"I know. But he's 13 only once."

"Yeah."

"Are you paying, or me?"

"I'll buy."

"What about the shirt with the Japanese writing?"

"You buy."

He returns with such remarkable timing that I'm wondering if he was listening right around the corner.

"We'll buy the parachute pants. But you've gotta take care of them. Understand?"

So we plop down the price of a nice pair of slacks plus $5 for something that looks like it came out of Michael Jackson's closet. And we pick up the shirt with Japanese writing.

That leaves us with just two things to do. First, we've got to make sure he can wear parachute pants to school. Then we must go shopping for something he can wear to fancy places.

But at least now you know how Ol' Boyd handles these things.

THE PRIDE OF MACON, GA

Plenty is said about Macon's cultural and historical ties and about how Macon tries to be one of the sophisticated kids of Georgia. But the real story of Macon is its people and their everyday struggles for health, hope and happiness. These are just a few of those stories.

Claude Winn:
A Complete Parent

One of life's little miracles happens every time a common person becomes uncommon.

Wars turn common men into heroes. All of us face little crises where
we have to bend or break, but we seldom have to be a hero. And we usually
survive.

Meet Claude Winn, a common man who became uncommon—the hard
way.

I like to talk about Claude. He's one of our own up in North Macon. He
was having a say about how the PTA was run before I knew there was a
North Macon, even long before I had a reason to join a PTA. He and his
early allies did a good job. We have a crackerjack PTA. Ask anyone who
knows about McKibben Lane School.

The school's PTA paid an overdue debt last month when it nominated
him as "Parent of the Year."

Friday, Claude won. I never had a doubt. You see, my friend is the true
parent—mother and father, sometimes sister and brother. For four years,
Claude has had to do it all. He lost his wife of 24 years in 1976.

It must have been a brutal awakening. After all, Claude was 50 with no
way to slow the years. And four children—at the time ranging in age from
9 to 18—left him with more responsibility than most men ever have to face.

But Claude is made of rare fiber. He grew up near Abbeville, S.C. His
father died before Claude was old enough to shave.

It should have surprised few people that Claude Winn carved out a comfortable niche in life. After all, he worked hard, trusted the Lord and
watched his nickels and dimes.

He came to Macon in 1963 from Savannah, a rising employee with a
dairy firm, Borden's Inc. He soon became general manager of the local
plant, a heady climb from his humble beginnings.

In the last 15 years, three of his children attended McKibben Lane School, and he's never been bashful about making suggestions for the betterment of all concerned. He'll battle for children in a heartbeat.

One of his sons borders on genius. He attends gifted classes at Lane. Claude has been an advocate of such classes.

The other son is mentally retarded. Claude battled just as hard for him. I believe it's because of the Claude Winns that we finally came out of the Dark Ages with handicapped people.

Outspoken Claude is the chairman of the governmental affairs committee of the Macon Association for Retarded Citizens. Which means he battles with everyone, including big-time politicians, to make things better for the handicapped. Thankfully, Claude Winn wins a lot of those battles.

The PTA folks figured Claude was the most deserving among nominees in Bibb County public schools. And they gave him a plaque at a luncheon Friday. Marvalene—who will become president of the McKibben Lane PTA Tuesday night—brought Claude by the office.

You'll never see a happier man. He was nattily attired in a three-piece suit, as usual. His gray hair was neatly combed, as usual. His smile was big and friendly, as usual.

In his hands, he clutched a plaque. There are others on his wall at home, but Claude said this one is the most important anyone ever gave him. And I like to believe it was awarded for doing what he's had to do best for the past four years—be a complete parent every day.

Claude sat in the office for a while Friday, talking about his family— Anne Ford, a nurse in the Neuro-Intensive Care Unit at the Medical Center of Central Georgia; Kathy Peavy, a kindergarten teacher; Kenneth, who competes in gymnastics and attends regular classes half a day despite being handicapped since birth; and Kevin, one of Lane's brightest students.

And Jennifer and Deedee, the two granddaughters in his life.

He said his tightly knit family "communicates every day and gets together real often."

In fact, he said he'd like to borrow a phone. A daughter was wondering how he scored.

Lilla Godfrey:
Prayer and a Dime

The hand that clutched mine still has remarkable strength. And when it isn't bracing its owner up on spindly legs, it still writes the familiar prayer and wraps the paper around a dime.

The voice is still strong and assertive, but a hearing problem sometimes makes it a one-way conversation.

But she's still on the move. With her 83rd birthday coming up April 20, Macon's "Prayer and a Dime Mother" keeps motivating.

I met her Monday. I read about her in the paper some years ago when then-Mayor Ronnie Thompson proclaimed her day in Macon.

Lately, I heard she gets the blues sometimes. That's why I visited her at Goodwill Nursing Home.

Lilla Godfrey said she was "young and scared" when she took that first hand-written prayer in 1941, wrapped it around a dime and pressed it into the hand of a serviceman heading for World War II.

She sent many prayers to thousands of serviceman in hopes that her two sons, Alva and Cecil, might return safely from that war. They did, and Alva Godfrey of Macon and Cecil Godfrey of Atlanta have brought her a lot of happiness—including seven grandchildren and eight great-grandchildren.

In 30 years, she sent more than 17,000 prayers that said, "I am praying for you wherever you go. Keep this always as a reminder to pray."

Those first dimes came from her grocery money, and at first her husband, R.A. Godfrey, did not know of the project. He found out about it when a serviceman took one of her gifts to *The Macon Telegraph*.

Once told, her story caught the imagination of a nation. Four presidents would commend her for her thoughtfulness and concern. Paramount News filmed her story and showed it all over the world. And her mailbag rivaled City Hall's.

She liked those letters and the words they contained. And she treasured the mementos that arrived from servicemen everywhere. In fact, she took her china out of its cabinet and put the mementos there for everyone to see.

In 52 years of marriage, the Godfreys engaged in numerous projects to help others, including sending ice cream to orphanages and academies for the blind on Mr. Godfrey's birthday each June 1.

After his death in 1971, she carried on—giving guitars to the blind, sending more prayers. . . .

Ill health slowed her down in recent years. Even with spinal problems, she lived in the neat little house at 726 Ponce de Leon Ave. well into her 80th year.

She moved into Goodwill Nursing Home in January of 1981. And she still carries on the Godfrey tradition of helping others.

She helps nursing home residents make stuffed animals that are sent to the Medical Center of Central Georgia to be given to youngsters as they come out of surgery.

She lives in a comfortable room at the end of a hallway and invites her company to sit and talk a spell. And when the company is ready to go, she searches around for a moment and then presses a small square of paper into a visitor's hand.

There seemed to be no need to ask what it was.

She kissed me on the cheek and said she sure would like for me to come back sometime. I think that's what Lilla Godfrey needs more than anything else—a little attention.

So I'm going to get a birthday card—something with pretty flowers on the front and touching words inside—and I'm going to address it to Mrs. Lilla Godfrey.

That's a pretty cheap price for a prayer and a dime.[1]

---

[1]Mrs. Godfrey died June 3, 1983, at age 83.

Papa Brown:
A Legend Grows

Don't strike out on this question, but do you really think baseball legends are built at Yankee Stadium and Candlestick Park?

No way. They're built on makeshift diamonds like the one Papa Brown laid out in his front yard eight years ago so a 2-year-old grandson could learn to run the bases.

Papa Brown knows what legends are all about. He grew up playing in the same area where Ty Cobb started baseball fires burning a generation before.

And 45 years later, he's the only coach I know who has snow-white hair, wears a back brace and still hits fly balls three or four times a week.

First time I ever saw the guy, I said, "What's an old fellow like you doing around a Little League field? Don't you know you could work up a cardiac arrest?"

Papa Brown took the ribbing with the same good-natured smile he offers the world every day. And I learned that our ballpark is a better place because he's there.

George I. Brown grew up in the hills of North Georgia, playing baseball for old Bowman High School, a few miles down a country road from Ty Cobb's homeplace. His daddy, the late W.W. Brown, played against Cobb for several years before the Detroit Tigers gave the "Georgia Peach" a big-league tryout.

Young George Brown played baseball through high school and also tried a little football "when you could fold up a football helmet and put it in your hip pocket."

He went to work after finishing high school in 1932, pushed baseball into the background and married a lady named Jenelle. They're still married 46 years later, and I consider that an indicator of the steadiness of Papa Brown.

He worked a variety of jobs in those early years before settling into a 28-year stint with Pure Oil Co. until his retirement four years ago.

Retirement . . . that's really what brought Papa Brown back to baseball. He had started his only "grandboy" on that diamond in his front yard some years before, and he had a job to finish.

At age 63, he returned to the baseball field as a coach.

What attracted me to Papa is that he's the kind of coach every parent wants for his or her child. In 66 years, the man in the Red Sox shirt has learned plenty about patience and tolerance, friendship and sportsmanship. And he obviously likes teaching it to the youngsters.

It's no secret that you have to be a gentleman—yes, even more important than being a good hitter—to play on Papa Brown's team.

He says he "never played ball with anyone I didn't like." And his philosophy dictates that players should play hard but still like one another.

He doesn't allow some practices that Little Leaguers often engage in. For instance, his players don't holler at the opposing batter; they encourage their pitcher.

Almost any Little Leaguer can tell you another thing about Papa Brown. Around him, a kid never goes thirsty.

"Some parents just bring their kids to the field and dump them off," he told me. That bothers him, but he never tells the kids.

He brings along a jug of Kool-Aid when he comes to the field. And he often supplements that with Cokes from the concession stand.

But the most amazing thing about Papa Brown is that he's undergone two major back operations—one in 1966 and another last winter—and still plays baseball with the boys.

"I can't squat down to catch for the boys like I used to, but I can do just about anything else," he said.

And why does he do it?

"Baseball is a good game. It builds character. We'll see some better men come out of all this."

Yes, maybe even a legend like Ty Cobb.

And in the meantime, Papa Brown is becoming something of a legend with the kids in North Macon.

The Saga
of Phillip Mann

I watched the muscled arm easily lift a 45-pound wheelchair into the back of the pickup. And then I watched a pair of skinny, withered, steel-braced legs begin a slow shuffle toward the cab of the truck.

Phillip Mann just finished another day's work. Unassisted, he had wheeled himself out of the Law Enforcement Center in Macon, lifted the small machine onto the big one, pulled his legs under the steering wheel by hand and driven away.

More than six years after he lost the use of his legs, Phillip Mann still earns his living, races a wheelchair five miles to raise money for a crippled children's hospital, and tells everyone who listens that he's really a very lucky man.

Instead of being a liability, Phillip is a plus mark, a victory sign, a symbol of accomplishment in our town.

Phillip Mann grew up in Macon wanting "to be a grownup more than anything else," he says. An internship with the Sheriff's Department while a senior at Mercer University spawned an interest in law enforcement. Soon after graduation, he became a deputy.

He'd married Elaine Hodges during his last year at Mercer and settled down to life as just an everyday man with a badge.

Until a February day in 1977 when a man he was guarding grabbed his gun and shot him twice. He was paralyzed from the waist down.

The early part of that comeback story has been told—rehabilitation at Shepherd Spinal Clinic in Atlanta, his return to the Sheriff's Department as a keeper of records, his first road race in a wheelchair in 1979.

But I thought it would be nice to catch up on this remarkable man.

Life in a wheelchair needs a strong foundation. Some folks never find it after tragedy strikes, but Phillip did.

● He found it in his family—a father, Joe, who spent countless hours with him during the rehabilitation period when he needed a father the most;

Elaine, the woman with endless patience and encouragement; a child, Jana, born just three months ago.

"I may never climb a tree with her (Jana), but I'm going to love her to death. I tell you, I hate to leave her to come to work in the morning."

● He found it in the people at the Bibb County Sheriff's Department, where people offer friendship and acceptance instead of pity and a constant helping hand.

"Lots of good people here. They treat me just like anyone else, and I doubt that they know how important that is to me."

● He found it in racing a lightweight wheelchair faster than many dedicated runners can run.

"Racing gives me a sense of freedom, a sense of accomplishment. The public will see me, and I know I'm not just doing something for myself. I feel like I'm doing something for everyone with a disability.

"What I like most about wheelchair sports is being around motivated people. I started taking tennis lessons this week. I wish more paraplegics would get into wheelchair sports."

● He found it in religion, and often takes his talks to church groups.

"I tell people I'm a pretty lucky fellow, and that I'd rather be a Christian in a wheelchair than a non-Christian walking around."

Last weekend, Phillip Mann traveled to Birmingham, Ala., and participated in a five-mile race for charity. And what was the charity?

"A real good cause," he says, "the crippled children's hospital in Birmingham."

And any time he passes through Atlanta, he makes sure he takes time to visit Shepherd Spinal Clinic and let others know that "there is life after spinal cord injuries."

He does these things despite relentless pain in his legs.

"Sure, I have pain. It's there all the time. It never leaves. I won't take Darvon because if I take two today, I know I'll need four tomorrow.

"Sometimes, the pain is so intense I can't sleep at night. And then there are times I don't want to get out of bed in the morning."

A smile played at the corners of his mouth. "But I'm going to walk down the road again someday. You can believe that. I'll do it . . . here or in heaven."

Helen Causey's Maimed Emotions

A wacko maimed some people's emotions Wednesday in Macon. He didn't hurt anyone on the outside. He just twisted up some innards, snarled some routines, brought some tears.

Helen Causey probably shouldn't have cried over a material thing like an automobile. But she did when she fell victim to some sorry character who torched six cars in parking lots Wednesday afternoon.

You really have to understand the car and the woman who owned it to see what a lowdown thing he did.

First off, Helen Causey is a typical struggling middle-aged American single person. A quick, crinkly smile is her most distinguishing feature. And anyone who can talk to her for a few minutes and not see the compassionate side of this woman . . . well, that person doesn't know beans about people.

Helen lives in a mobile home in South Macon and tries to keep her bills paid on take-home pay of less that $200 a week. She wears her hair pinned high and a ring bearing the birthstones of those closest to her.

One of the nice things in her life was the 1975 Chevy Caprice she bought a little over two years ago. Her son, Allen, said it was a solid, dependable machine. As it turned out, he was right.

For two years, Helen Causey made out a check every month for $99.30 to pay for it. Two months ago, she made the last payment.

Yes, it was a good car. It took her four miles to work at the Zayre store on Eisenhower Parkway five days a week.

On weekends, it took her to Warner Robins and Milledgeville to see a brother or sister. It hauled grandchildren just about every place grandchildren ask to go.

Until last April, it carried Helen to Goodwill Nursing Home where her mother lived for nine years.

And after her mother's death, it carried a homemade doll with homemade clothes in the front seat, a special doll made by her mother.

Besides being a good luck charm, it made Helen feel like her mother was still near.

The blue and white Chevy never broke down on her. That's because the folks in the maintenance shop at the rear of the store where she works took care of it. Just last week, she paid $36.17 for a tuneup.

She parked it as usual Wednesday morning, the homemade doll in the front seat.

The next time Helen saw the car, flames were shooting 25 feet into the air. A wacko probably stood off to one side and got his jollies watching the fire. It took that kind of sick mind to do that dirty deed.

Helen cried while policemen, firemen and reporters were there.

She went home that night and cried alone. But Allen told her everything would be all right, that they'd get the insurance money—whatever the amount—and he'll help her find another car every bit as good as the Chevy.

By Friday afternoon, Helen had that crinkly smile going again. She told me that she knew a little bit about how people felt when their homes burned. She said it makes a person feel just about as empty as a soul can feel.

Her special "family" at the Zayre store, her son, her daughter-in-law, two grandchildren—those folks had her feeling almost human again.

But I couldn't resist asking this gentle woman how she felt about justice for the wacko who set the fire. What would she deem appropriate?

She said she'd like to set a little part of him on fire, like maybe his fanny, and let it burn for "just a minute" before putting it out.

I told her I'd hold the son-of-a-gun while she struck a match. I'd do that just thinking about a homemade doll that had burned to a crisp.

BEST IN
THE BOONDOCKS

*A needle suspended over a woman's wrist can predict
the sex of an unborn child? 'Possum in a pan is good
eating? Since 1973, the rural folks have shared love
stories and superstitions, recipes and heartbreak with
me. This is the way they told the stories.*

Shadrack Ware: Forever Young

JEFFERSONVILLE—If I didn't know the guy and like him, I could feel a little jealous of Shadrack Ware. After all, I'm 43, going on 75. Shadrack is 75, going on 43.

Undoubtedly, the man has found the fountain of youth. But, instead of jealousy at such a find, I just admire Shadrack for the life he leads.

I could write a book about Shadrack Ware.

Shadrack became my friend more than four years ago when I was attracted to his neat little home on Bullard Road in Twiggs County by a fantastic array of yellow flowers in the front yard.

A straight and tall man answered my knock and said those were Anna's flowers. But Anna, his wife of more than 52 years and mother of his 12 children, couldn't be in a photograph. She had "gone on to heaven."

So he tended the flowers alone.

Shadrack told me what life was like without Anna. With time on his hands, he did more for others.

He told me he once made a promise to himself about helping others, and he's still keeping that promise—every day of his life.

"I didn't make the promise to the Almighty God." He smiled and said, "He knows what I'm doing. I just told myself that I would do these things for others."

Shadrack was born near Dry Branch, the son of a bricklayer. At age 19, he went to the industrial North to seek a higher paying job than a black man could expect to land in rural Georgia in the 1920s.

After several years in Philadelphia and Camden, N.J., he finally settled in New York City. At first, he took any job that would turn an honest buck. He once worked for a junkyard and drove a horse and wagon through New York picking up scrap metal.

He worked his way into the building trades, always trying to make more money for his growing family. Finally, the sporadic employment in construction made him seek more consistent employment as a baker.

When that didn't pay all of the bills, he managed a 60-unit apartment complex on the side. I guess you see what I'm getting at—Shadrack Ware always made his way.

Shadrack did something else, too. Every one of the Ware children graduated from high school and several went on to college. One of them, Latresa Beck, is a registered nurse in New York City. Another, Justine Strickland, holds a master's degree in education and teaches in Denver.

One son died of wounds received in World War II. The other 11 children have been a constant source of pride for Shadrack Ware. "I'm so proud of them . . . and I know they're proud of me. Yes, life has been very good to me."

After 38 years as a baker, Shadrack retired in 1965. Six years later, he moved back to Georgia to get away from the high crime rate in big cities. "The crime . . . life is double rough in big cities. A man can get enough of that kind of life."

Shadrack told me he's a Jehovah's Witness, but the title he put on his religion seems unimportant. A preacher would have a hard time equalling Shadrack's deeds.

When Shadrack got back to Georgia, he was surprised to find so many people—especially so many elderly black people near his homeplace—who don't own a car, don't drive or won't drive for various reasons.

He brought a 1965 Ford to Georgia with him. He retired it last year with 106,000 miles on it, most of them for someone else. He bought a 1977 Granada, and it's getting plenty of miles.

"But there's no bus service out here, and many of these folks have no way of getting to the doctor's office or to town to shop."

Shadrack Ware takes them, accepting only a few dollars to keep the car on the go.

Shadrack's little home has been a stopping point for me, a place to cool my heels and drink cold well water.

And, when I leave, I always feel like I have things in a better perspective. A man like Shadrack Ware does that for people.

Benjie Zeigler's Old Wives' Tale

WARNER ROBINS—Benjie Zeigler is my kind of people. She's easy-going, kind-hearted, and just about as country as anyone I know.

Her worst habit is smoking a pack a day. The worst word I've ever heard her say is "durn."

But Benjie spends so much of her time helping others that you don't notice those other things. Especially since she takes care of two kids, a husband and a job besides doing her good deeds.

I met Benjie when she was trying to help someone. She's manager of a Nu-Way Restaurant in Warner Robins, and she was raising money to help a waitress who had been injured in an auto accident.

Since then, we've shared a few conversations with coffee on the side. We each had a cup in front of us one day last week when she dropped her bombshell.

"Would you believe I'm pregnant?"

"You can't be. You're too old for that sort of thing."

"Durned if that's so. I ain't but 28."

"That's too old."

"You'd better not say that again."

A customer leaving the restaurant interrupted us. "Hi, Benjie. How are you?"

"Pregnant," I said before Benjie could answer. I didn't catch the guy's expression. Benjie was talking again.

"Listen," she said, "I'm going to have a girl."

"You're really something today, Benjie. First, you say you're not too old to be having a baby, and now you tell me you're going to have a girl. Does knowledge like that come from being an older woman?"

"Listen, you keep talking about that older woman stuff, and I'm gonna hit you a lick that'll knock you into next Sunday."

"Don't get violent. Just tell me how you know you're going to have a girl."

"Easy. I use a needle and thread."

"Needle and thread?"

"Sure. You just hold it over the pulse in a woman's wrist. If it swings in a circle, it'll be a girl, and if it swings across the wrist, it'll be a boy."

"Hey, that's an old wives' tale."

"So what? It works."

"Bull."

"No bull. C'mon, I'll show you."

She led me to the back of the restaurant. The waitresses all smiled knowingly when Benjie asked, "Where's the needle and thread?"

"You keep it here?"

"Sure, I've told everyone how many children they have—or will have. It works both ways, you know."

"And you were right?"

"Every time."

She found the needle and thread. "Watch," she said. I couldn't have looked the other way if I'd wanted to.

She wrapped the thread around her wrist one time and then pulled upward. The dangling needle began a circular motion. "A girl," she said. "That's the first child I had."

She did it again. This time it swung sharply across her wrist. "A boy. That's my second child."

Again she pulled. It swung across her wrist again. "Another boy."

"Wait. That's four children. Are you going to have still another?"

"Gene said if this one's a girl, he'll still want a boy. I guess that would make four, wouldn't it?"

"But you'd be so. . . ."

"Say 'old,' and I'll clobber you."

"Benjie, you don't really believe that needle and thread stuff, do you?"

"Of course not. It's just an old wives' tale."

Then she smiled like a fox. Benjie knows something. But the best I can do is wait for December to find out for sure.

And if it's a girl, I'll be the only one who ever ate crow at a Nu-Way.[2]

---

[2] Sure enough, Benjie bore a girl, Sherry Jean, who was born Nov. 15, 1983.

Laverne Griffin's 'Possum in a Pan

GORDON—All the way to Gordon, I was thinking that Laverne Griffin's cooking stories would have my pal Muley grinning like a 'possum eating briars.

When you say "country cooking," Muley will sit down at your table so quick you'll think he's your brother-in-law. But he won't be sitting at Laverne's table when she cooks her most famous dish—opossum.

Muley's eyebrows went skyward when I said something about eating 'possum. "Nope. Not me. No, sir. Never." I've never heard Muley be so emphatic.

My taste buds rank 'possum right down there with squid, turtles and frog legs, but I thought Muley would like it.

Personally, I never knew 'possum served any useful purpose.

Some kids in Wilkinson County once told me that a 'possum makes a great Frisbee after it lays in the road a couple of weeks and hundreds of tires have flattened it out.

But I'd count that as being useful only if you live in Wilkinson County and mom won't take you to town for a real Frisbee.

Laverne Griffin insists that 'possum is great eating. She even told me how to cook it. But she's also told the whole world how to cook it.

Her recipe for cooking this critter first appeared in the Macon Telegraph and News Cookbook in 1974. Since then, she's been contacted by lots of people to expound on—and lend credence to—that recipe.

Just a few weeks ago, a writer in Vancouver, Wash., called and said he wanted to tell people how to beat economic hard times. He figured one way was to eat more 'possum and Laverne's recipe might help. People in Vancouver obviously don't know that 'possums make great Frisbees.

Anyhow, Laverne sat in her kitchen this week and told me about herself and that recipe.

Her father died when she was 7, she said, and times were hard. So her family learned to live off what they could grow in a garden and the game they could trap in nearby pine forests.

And she practically memorized every recipe her grandmother had, including one for oppossum.

Here's the way Laverne says to prepare and cook a 'possum.

"First, you pen him up for three or four weeks and feed him table scraps and buttermilk. A 'possum eats almost anything when he runs wild, so first, you need to clean him out.

"When he's ready, you kill him by hitting him behind the head with a board. Don't shoot him. That might spoil the meat.

"Then you cut him open and scald him just like you would a pig. Now you're ready to cook him. So you par-boil him."

I held up my hand. I didn't know what "par-boil" meant.

"That means you boil him 'til he's half done. Then you put him in a baking dish and put potatoes around him. That makes the dish pretty. You whip up some batter with flour and hot pepper and vinegar, and you baste the 'possum as it bakes.

"You keep sprinkling the water from the 'possum onto the potatoes to give them a 'possum taste. You do all this while you cook him at 400 degrees for an hour."

Just about that time, her husband Billy walked in. I asked him if he likes 'possum. His nose sort of turned up and he said, "I tried it once . . . just once . . . that was enough."

I can see Billy and I are going to be great friends. I wonder if he plays Frisbee?

Quadruplets:
1 . . . 2 . . . 3 . . . 4 . . .

Quadruplets.

Just the word quickens the pulse. It makes me want to cheer loudly for motherhood.

But I have to wonder how Robin Cochran Baggett will cope over, say, the next 20 years.

I keep thinking . . . four bottles of formula to mix . . . four baths to give . . . four pacifiers to keep in place . . . a four-seat stroller to push. . . .

When four colds need doctoring, will that happy smile remain?

When four bikes are needed at Christmas or one tux and three gowns at prom time, can she keep motivating?

With four kids in school and then college—all at once—can she balance the checkbook?

She says she will.

Questions about Brad and Brandi and Becki and Betti could go on forever. I asked Robin, a native of Roberta, to tell me what it's like for a family to jump from two to six members in less than an hour.

She talked about "plans" that emerged in $2\frac{1}{2}$ years of marriage to Warren Baggett, a Dublin native.

"We always said we'd like to have two children, a boy and a girl. We never dreamed we'd get a boy and a girl . . . and a girl . . . and a girl . . . all at one time."

"Doctors told me at first that I was going to have twins. Then I was told on March 1 there would be three.

"They made more X-rays after I went in to the hospital. And while I was in labor, the doctor told me, 'Now, Mrs. Baggett, I want you to take me serious. We have four babies in there.' No one had mentioned that word to me until right then.

"I think I went into shock. Isn't that something? I was in labor and shock at the same time."

Her laugh was a happy one. After all, if those doctors kept coming back . . . well, for a young woman who was an only child and talked about having just two children, four babies are plenty, thank you.

There were some complications. The babies were premature and small—so small that doctors would normally give them just a 1-in-4 chance of surviving. But Robin told me Thursday that all four "are coming along real well."

The health of the children is her main concern, she said, but she looked briefly at the future.

Hospital bills—"The only estimate I've heard is that care is costing about $1,500 a day. (All costs may run as high as half a million dollars before the quads are completely on their own.)

Insurance coverage—"So far, it looks like the bills will be paid."

Income—"Warren can probably support us, but that's about all. Money will be tight. I don't know what I'll do about going back to work. When the doctors said triplets, I checked around. Day care was going to cost us $100 a week for just three babies."

Retrospect—"If I could go back? I wouldn't have said I wanted four babies, but now that I have them, I wouldn't take anything in the world for them."

Endorsements—"People tell me that diaper and formula companies might be interested. But right now, I just want to get them home."

Even though all four little Baggetts came into the world within an hour, there's sure to be the usual family roles.

For instance, Brad was the first-born and the only boy. He's destined to be his daddy's shadow.

The "baby" of the babies is Betti, and her mother acknowledges that she's sure to be the spoiled one. She's named for her maternal grandmother, Betty Cochran. The other three have the curly golden locks of their father, but Betti has straight black hair like Mrs. Cochran.

"I'm sure she won't want for attention from her grandmother," Robin said.

In other words, the Baggetts are going to have a very normal family despite the ballyhoo of children that are born only once in every 60,000 births.[3]

---

[3]One of the quadruplets, Becki, died June 17, 1982, of respiratory problems.

Bessie Mae Turner's Love Story

HILLSBORO—I have a love story that will open those sleepy Monday morning eyes, dear reader. It's about a bride who attended her husband's funeral almost five years before they were married.

You may remember Bessie Mae White Turner. A month ago, I wrote about her class of 1922 having a reunion. But stories about this charming woman abound. Read on:

Bessie Mae was just 12 when word came back to this tiny Jasper County town that Donald Brooks Turner, a machine-gunner fighting World War I, had died in action.

Since bodies often were buried on the battlefield in that war, Hillsboro planned an immediate funeral service for its fallen hero. Banks of flowers decorated the sanctuary of Hillsboro Methodist Church, and people filled every pew.

And young Bessie Mae "cried my eyes out."

After the service, she helped carry the flowers to the home of a sister of the "dead" soldier.

A cablegram came six months later saying the soldier was indeed alive. He sent it himself after reading his obituary in the county newspaper.

When he came home, he lived with his sister next door to Bessie Mae. Over the next couple of years, he fell in love with her and asked her to marry him. But she was 14. She said she'd have to finish school first.

She graduated in May of 1922, and they were married on Dec. 31. But Bessie May calls it "a May-December wedding" for more reasons than those dates. At the time, she was 17 and he was 38.

"Some people thought it was terrible, that young girl and that old man getting married. But he was so young in spirit.

"I had no regrets. Never. Getting married so young might not be all right for everyone. I guess it would depend on the person. But it was all right for me."

They spent their honeymoon night in Room 308 of the Dempsey Hotel in Macon, and she recalls watching the festive, noisy New Year's celebration from the hotel window.

"When I turned away from the window, I stepped on my husband's sock supports. You don't remember celluloid sock supports, but men wore them back then. They didn't let their socks fall down around their ankles like they do today.

"Well, I was so upset. I said, 'Mr. Brooks. . . .' He was so much older than me that I called him Mr. Brooks for the first 15 years we were married . . . until I got a little older. I said, 'Mr. Brooks, I believe I stepped on your sock supports and broke them.'

"He just hugged and kissed me and told me not to worry my pretty little head about them, that he'd buy some more.

"Four years later, one of our boys was having a nightmare and I was trying to get to his bed. I stepped on another pair and broke them. That time, he said, 'Why don't you watch where the hell you're going?'

"I started laughing and he said, 'What are you laughing at?' I said, 'Well, I was just thinking about how much difference four years can make.' I like to tell that story to young folks who are about to get married so they know how things change."

Fifty-five years after that first funeral, she went to another. The couple had been married 51 years, brought three sons into the world and weathered even the hardest of times.

"We didn't always agree on everything, but we never broke up, never talked about divorce like people do today. . . ."

Bessie Mae will turn 78 in September, and she needs a cane to get around. But she still knows how to get a man's attention.

"Say, I've got some collard greens and peas on the stove, baked sweet potatoes, corn bread and apple cobbler. . . ."

Answering Fools' Questions

JEFFERSONVILLE—Brian Floyd doesn't have a contagious disease. He doesn't contaminate.

His hair fell out because he takes chemotherapy treatments to fight leukemia.

I wanted to get that out of the way first. You see, some people back away from Brian as if he has the plague. Others laugh and point at him. Still others ask tacky questions.

Naturally, this makes Brian feel self-conscious.

Kids are bad enough at this sort of thing. But some older people get thoughtless and careless, too.

Last weekend, Brian Floyd finally had enough. He asked his mom to buy him a wig. It's a darn cruel world that makes a 3-year-old come up with an idea like that.

Brian's fight isn't easy, even with Twiggs County folks cheering him on and donating money to help defray expenses for his many trips to a special hospital.

Every few weeks—or sometimes, several weeks in a row—Brian and his mom make a grueling 11-hour trek to St. Jude's Hospital in Memphis. It takes that long to drive to the Macon airport, fly to Atlanta, make connections to Memphis, get a taxi to the hospital and finally settle into a motel room.

That wouldn't be so bad except that Beulah Floyd gets a little scared.

She's always scared for Brian, afraid the medical news might get worse instead of better.

She's scared of planes. She said she never flew in a plane—or ever ventured out of Georgia—until that first trip to Memphis just over a year ago.

And she's scared of Memphis because Dudley Floyd, Brian's dad, must stay in Georgia and work the kaolin mines to keep the family away from total financial disaster. Beulah faces the noisy city, the fearful streets and the lonely nights without the security of having a husband at her side.

But she keeps going because chemotherapy lets Brian live a little while longer. And she keeps facing the unknowing fools almost every day who make a little boy self-conscious.

Beulah Floyd says she will never get used to airplanes. Every time the plane descends, she holds Brian with one arm and one of those sick bags with the other. If you've got to fly, you wouldn't want Beulah's stomach.

You can see why my friend always is glad to set her feet on the ground in Macon and head for the brick home at the edge of Jeffersonville.

She likes the hugs from Dudley and Chuckie, 10, and the comfort of her own home. She can sip coffee with friends in a kitchen decorated with a collection of baskets and ceramic wall plaques she made.

She can drive to her friendly supermarket and get the kind of food she wants and prepare it her way to feed two sons and a husband.

And she can get up in the morning and drive the school bus that earns a few more dollars for the family bank account. . . .

That's where the cruelty really started, she said.

"Maybe I stared at the kids the first time I went to the hospital, but I hope not. It's so common up there that no one seems to think about it.

"But the kids on the school bus started one morning. They had a party off Brian. They laughed and . . . Oh, I get mad everytime I think about it. I wanted to turn a few of them across my lap. But I didn't.

"And Brian . . . he didn't pay any attention at first. He just went on playing and jumping around."

But that was just a beginning to the awful tackiness. The young mother noticed more and more how people stared and reacted stupidly to Brian's appearance—as recently as a shopping trip last weekend.

"If they want to know, I don't mind them asking. But staring and drawing back like they might catch something . . . that's what I can't take."

Now, Brian notices, too.

So we get down to what Ol' Boyd has to say.

If you ever laughed at someone with a disfigurement, a stutter or stammer, or a crippling walk. . . .

If you ever called anyone a name because of skin color. . . .

If you ever asked a thoughtless question that hurt someone and didn't apologize. . . .

If you ever let a smart mouth ruin somebody's day. . . .

If you've done any of these things, you need a change in habits.

If you know someone who does this sort of thing, save this column for that nut. Or just tell why a little boy in Jeffersonville thinks he needs to wear a wig.[4]

---

[4]Brian died on Feb. 18, 1983, of leukemia.

80 AND OVER . . . AND BEAUTIFUL

In my early days of reporting, I'd stop at a nursing home if there was nothing else to do. And sure enough, someone would tell me a story worth the space in a good newspaper. Problem is, I fell in love with a whole generation of people. That's why there's an 80-and-Over Happy Birthday Club that has printed more than 1,400 birthdays in just two years. That's why there was a birthday party that drew 1,800 the very first time around. And that's why I can offer a lifetime warranty on the stories in this chapter.

How It All Started

This is about how you get your name in the paper. If you've wondered how you can do that honorably, all you have to do from now on is live to age 80 and write to me.

A letter that arrived in the Mother's Day letter-writing contest started me thinking about how people get their names in the paper.

A lady wrote that, even if she didn't win a free dinner for her mother, she was sure her mother would be happy just to see her name in print. Her mother, an elderly woman, only sees her name in the paper when she is listed as a surviving relative in an obituary, said the writer.

Some bright soul once said that everyone likes to see his or her name in print. And that's certainly true. But do you know when a name is most likely to appear?

First, when a person is born.

Big deal. A baby lies there in a crib, sleeping and gooing, and his name's in the paper. When the kid is 10, his mother collars him while he's searching for his baseball glove to show him the clipping. He thinks she's lost her marbles, so he shrugs and goes back to looking for the mitt.

Second most likely time: When a person dies. The name appears in large letters, "Mr. Doe," the headline says. And the smaller type says Mr. Doe's relatives are gathering at the local Baptist church to pay their respects.

About five years ago, someone on the Telegraph had the idea of printing "First Birthday" pictures. And those little guys and gals sure are cute.

But do they know what's going on? Never. I mean, you show the picture to the little tyke and say, "Look, Napoleon. Your picture's in the paper!"

And what does the kid do? He slobbers on it. So Mom wipes it dry and packs it away to show him when he's 10 and searching for a ball glove.

There are other ways the average person can see his or her name in print. Get a divorce. Rob a store. Have a wreck. Get a gun permit . . . naw, forget that one. Anyhow, the list doesn't sound very enticing.

But Ol' Boyd is changing things a little—for those 80 and older. They can get their name in the paper right here in this column.

And by the way, we have one name for this week. A letter from Phyllis W. Williams, a regular reader in Byron wants to nominate her mother. So here it is:

Cynthia P. Williams of Helena, 85, May 30.

It's
Party Time

A lady called me last week and asked, "You're really having a party for 1,800 people?"

"If that many show up," I said.

"Good Lord, aren't you nervous?"

"No."

"I'd be going into cardiac arrest," she said.

Ordinarily, I don't let that sort of thing throw me. But 1,800 people?

It finally dawned on me Friday afternoon that almost 2,000 people were going to come to the Macon Coliseum for a party I'd dreamed up.

I stared out the window and wondered how far a line of 1,800 people would reach. To Gray? Not hardly. Then to the Macon Coliseum from my office? Yes, surely that far.

In my mind's eye, I could see the line. And I drifted off into whatever people drift into when they might have bitten off more than they can chew. I felt that way when I took my first chew of tobacco.

It never dawned on me to just leave town. No, sir, I kept answering phone calls and praying that people like Jim Plunkett, Linda Wheeler and Dave Wallace knew what they were doing.

I prayed that Ray Melton and his orchestra, the Merrimakers and the Wings of Harmony would show up.

I prayed that Zell Miller, Roy Rowland and George Israel would be there.

I prayed the door prizes wouldn't get ripped off sitting out there in my van.

I forgot to pray that the guests would show up.

But they came. Some were there when the doors opened at noon. They got to listen to the band tune instruments and watch the finishing touches being put on a setting of 220 tables and 1,200 balloons.

I need not have worried. There was a lot of scurrying and a lot of hustle, but the party went together like we'd done it a hundred times.

A few minutes before 1 p.m., I paused and looked around.

Ray Melton and the orchestra were playing songs that bring back memories of waltzing and dancing in a grand ballroom.

About 60 young folks—smart, sharp, helpful young people who belong to the Junior Civitan and Junior Civinette Clubs at Southwest High School—were everywhere. Their presence removed a little cloud of worry from over my head.

And the 40 or so friends and co-workers who spent their Sunday afternoon helping just for the sake of helping reminded me of the good folks I rub elbows with every day.

No, I need not have worried. I really had no time for worry.

For four hours, I emceed the show. . . . I made a couple of dozen announcements and missed a couple of dozen more. (Sorry about that, folks.) I signed my name a couple of hundred times (and wondered why in the world anyone would want my autograph).

I introduced some of the finest people I know to some of the finest people in all of Middle Georgia.

In between, I tried to visit every table in the place. (I failed miserably. Sorry again, folks.)

Finally, the door prizes were gone, and everyone was heading home.

That's when the tiny woman said she'd been trying to catch me all afternoon. Then she reached up and put her arms around my neck and whispered in my ear.

"Tell Marvalene not to be jealous," she said. "I'm 94 and can't be very dangerous at that age. I just wanted to tell you that I may not be here next year. But I had a wonderful, wonderful time this year . . . yes, a wonderful time."

And she kissed me on the cheek.

That said it all. I don't think about packing and leaving town anymore.

But I had to stand there and wait for a lump in my throat to go away so I could tell Marvalene that I was starving, that my appetite had just returned.

Next year, I won't worry a bit.

Herbert and Clemmie: Luckiest Couple

MONTROSE—Name the luckiest couple you know. Name someone with every reason to be really thankful this week of Thanksgiving. And then I want to tell you about my choice—Herbert and Clemmie Bridges.

Just sitting down in the living room of their little frame home and listening to these folks is the kind of experience that makes me feel like skipp-ity-do-da-ing down a country lane to a big farmhouse for a family reunion with dinner on the ground.

Herbert and Clemmie are family. They're the best kind of family. Come next Jan. 6, they will have been married 60 years.

Sixty years. And they've all been good ones.

Consider this:

- They brought nine children into this world.
- Their children brought them 35 grandchildren.
- Their grandchildren brought them 52 great-grandchildren.
- And so far, their great-grandchildren have brought them four great-great-grandchildren.

Lucky? Yessiree. Any way you count it that's 100 offspring and every one is still alive except a 10-year-old great-granddaughter who died several years ago in a car wreck.

And Herbert and Clemmie Bridges just might get to see every one of them during this holiday season. They'll come from as far away as Michigan and Texas, because they're the kind of kin who like to visit. All nine children and dozens of others were on hand for a family reunion in September.

Life won't get much better than the holiday season at the little frame home on a quiet street at the southeast edge of Montrose.

Herbert Lugene Bridges was born on a farm near Dudley in 1898. He left Georgia in 1917 to fight in World War I. He clearly recalls the rigors of war—losing 20 pounds in three months on the front line and lying wounded in the Argonne Forest just a few days before Armistice Day in 1918.

He married Clemmie Lillion Lord of Washington County on Jan. 24, 1924. They'd met because his first cousin was married to her sister.

He got out of the Army in November of 1924 and returned to Georgia. For 20 years, he worked in sawmills and farmed on the side as his family quickly expanded—Lillie Mae, Mable, Ruth, Mogarette, Doris, Gene, Patsy, Mary and J.R.

In 1943, he started working in civil service and retired 18 years later from Robins Air Force Base. But he kept farming on the side—hogs, cows, row crops and whatever else was needed—to feed his large family.

"We may not have had everything we wanted," says Clemmie, "but we had everything we needed."

She paused a moment and then said, "The Lord blessed us to raise all of the children . . . and feed them all . . . and keep them all healthy while they were growing up. Yes, sir, the Lord's been good to us, real good."

Ask Herbert and Clemmie Bridges about their life together, and the answers are as honest and uncomplicated as their lifestyle.

How have they survived 60 years under the same roof?

"Love," says Herbert with the intensity of an old-time preacher, "is what keeps people together. Won't nothing else do it."

And are they still in love?

"Oh, yes," he says earnestly. "We're together, aren't we?"

And what causes broken marriages?

"People live too fast. And they're not as happy today as we used to be. Maybe that's because there is so much meanness in the world."

What's the subject they most often differed on?

"The grocery bill," he says.

"Yes," she said, giving him a smile even as she disagreed, "but we have plenty."

And I think they still do.

Grandma Walker: She's Huggable

McRAE—The road to Grandma Walker's house is just like I expected it to be—a dirt, single-lane driveway between neatly plowed fields where 10-foot corn grows in summer.

And Grandma Walker—she turned 80 when the corn was ripening last October—is just the kind of person you and I learn to love at first sight.

Forget the gals of the jiggly generation for a moment. They'll break your pocketbook and your heart—sometimes in that order.

Not Grandma Walker. The worse she'll do is feed you those garden vegetables and farm-grown meat until you bust. Folks like her make you yearn for a weekend in the country.

Not long ago, I guided the family car down the dirt driveway to Grandma's house for a family dinner. Nothing fancy, you understand. Just good food and good conversation.

Now, Grandma isn't one of *the* Walkers—you know, Wimbric, Jack and Ronnie, the super politicos of Telfair County.

Grandma is one of the other Walkers, widow of Fred Walker who worked the same fields many a year before he passed on 10 years ago.

Her children, Robert, Howard, Jimmy and Elizabeth, never ran for public office. They've always been too busy slopping the hogs and planting corn. Just plain folks, honest and unobtrusive.

Several things about Ellen Elizabeth Walker impressed me.

First, she's survived 80 years in this world, taking what it had to offer with a grain of salt and the Lord's prayer.

Second, there isn't much about cooking that Grandma doesn't know. You know that the first time you sit down to her table. It's always covered with the best in vegetables and fresh meat—maybe 90 percent coming from her farm.

And third, she's huggable. The dictionary doesn't list the word; I invented it just for her. It means—just in case Webster wants to list it—that she's typical grandma material.

Kids love her at first sight. They hug her, hang on her, adore her. And kids don't lie about their affections. That's why she's huggable.

We ate enough food to traverse the Sahara Desert without a refill, and then we went for a walk. Grandma says it's good "to let your food settle."

We walked down another dirt road, and I found out still more about Grandma. She's no gypsy. She lives a mile from where she was born, and that's as far away as she's ever taken up permanent residence.

On that sunny afternoon, she showed me the house I hadn't seen before—a weather-beaten structure nestled among giant shade trees. It takes me back to my childhood, to the house I lived in 35 years ago.

Lizzie—that's what her friends call her—and Fred Walker lived in that house for most of her 80 years. Her father-in-law built it in 1890. Three of her four children were born there.

Three porches line different sides of the house. A well—"We drew many a bucket of water out of there"—is covered now. Feed for the hogs is stored inside the old house.

But I'd still sleep there on a stormy night. The roof looks like it can handle it. The doorknob and ancient slip-latch have been worn shiny by happy hands.

Grandma Walker sat on the porch and said, "This is the coldest house in the world." And then she smiled, adding a warmth that maybe she never noticed. But we did.

One relative laughed at the memory and said, "This is the house with the four rooms and a path instead of eight rooms and a bath."

Even Grandma laughed at that.

Cars coming in the driveway broke the reverie. More people to be fed. She pulled herself up on the cane, and walked back up the road, past the hog pens and towering oaks.

Memories are fine with Grandma Walker. But when folks show up with the hungries, she's the queen of the kitchen. Even after 80 years.

Miss Cleo:
The Baseball Fan

HAWKINSVILLE—Remember Ty Cobb? Cleo Roberts does.

That takes a lot of remembering, but Miss Cleo can do it because she's lived almost 100 years.

Because his baseball career ended in 1928, maybe you really didn't know Ty Cobb. And unless you lived around Winder, you probably never heard of Cleo Roberts.

But Miss Cleo always thrived on baseball—from Ty Cobb to Phil Niekro.

She spent many weekend afternoons watching Cobb, her brother and other northeast Georgians play baseball at the turn of the century.

In her autumn years, she's confined to a wheelchair. But she's confined in a dignified sort of way. When you talk to her, you know you're talking to a lady—a lady with a touch of angelic devilment, but a lady nonetheless.

The first time I opened my mouth to her, she said, "Say what? I look more than 100? Did you really say that? My goodness, what a thing to say."

I sat there with my mouth hanging open, hoping with all my heart that I really hadn't said that.

Then she rescued me. She smiled and added, "It's all right. I forgive you."

Such was my introduction to Miss Cleo's sense of humor.

On a sun porch at Pinewood Manor, Cleo Evanson Roberts shared a view across a lake and some of her 100 years. She was born April 2, 1881, in Elbert County. She married a store clerk named Paul Roberts and she bore him two daughters.

But before she fell for Paul Roberts, she fell for baseball. Her brother Arthur, who aspired to the big leagues, too, introduced her to Ty Cobb.

Arthur never made the big leagues. "I remember my father telling Arthur, 'If you start thinking you can make a living playing baseball like that fellow Ty Cobb, I'll disinherit you.' We laughed about it and asked him, 'Disinherit Arthur from what?'"

Miss Cleo reared two daughters, but she never had a son to thrill her on the baseball field. "If God had ever given me a son, I would have made a baseball player out of him. . . .

"But I had a grandson who said he wanted to be a baseball player. And I spent—oh, my goodness—it must have been $10 or more for a glove. And you know what? If he ever threw a baseball 40 feet, I never knew about it."

So she did the next best thing. She adopted a baseball team—the Atlanta Braves, a team born when she was more than 80. And when she was 95, they adopted her, naming her the team "grandmother."

She gets to the games now and then, and she has a standing invitation from Ted Turner to attend, including a trip up the elevator to the VIP boxes.

Cap'n Ted isn't dumb. Miss Cleo is probably the best public relations thing he has going.

Who else is pushing 100 and riding around in a wheelchair with a Braves bumpersticker that reads "Wait till THIS year"?

Never doubt that Cleo Roberts is an avid fan. She ticks off player after player on her fingers, reciting the trades that helped and those that hurt. In other words, she's a home run hitter in the hot-stove league.

Her favorite players are Phil Niekro and Dale Murphy. And when the Braves visited Macon Mall last month, she was right there, pen in hand and chasing Niekro in her wheelchair.

For more than an hour, we talked. And when I started to leave, she said I needed a kiss. Make that two kisses, one on each cheek, she added.

Then she said, "You forgot to ask how a person lives to 100."

So I asked.

"Get to 99 and then be real careful," she said.

Her audience broke up.[5]

---

[5]Miss Cleo died April 14, 1982, at age 101. She did not get to see her Braves win 13 games in a row at the start of the 1982 season and go on to win a division title.

MY PAL MULEY

Muley. The name is magic. He can whip a quadruple bypass quicker than you can say ham hocks, okra and blackeyed peas. He can spin a yarn better than anyone I ever knew . . . and get people to believe him, too. And when he fails to bail me out of blank-minded Monday mornings, you'll see me hopping a freight to Yankeeland.

Nobody's Invincible, Not Even Muley

Why have I always believed that my heroes are invincible? Just foolishness, huh?

I felt that way about Daddy Philpot, the stepdaddy who raised me. Just take my word that one kid thought his stepdaddy would live forever.

John Wayne looked like a rock. I thought he'd live forever.

They're both gone.

I believed my pal Muley was invincible, too. What can possibly hurt a country boy with a laid-back attitude and a skin as tough as any alligator?

But we almost lost him Thursday.

How many people have asked me if Muley is real? A hundred? Five hundred? A thousand? More?

I keep saying, yeah, Muley is real.

Yeah, he's so real he had a heart attack smack-dab in the middle of the workday, sitting right there at his desk.

When someone told me that Muley was sick, I thought maybe he'd gotten ragweed mixed up with turnip greens.

We'd had a cup of coffee 15 minutes ago, I thought, and he'd looked fine. Besides, Muley is too young—just 52—to be very sick.

Maybe a Bloody Mary for lunch would get him right. Muley never drinks at lunch, but we could change the routine one time.

When I walked into his office my pal had his head propped on his hands.

"Hey, Muley, you OK?" I asked.

He looked up. His face was the color of yesterday's ashes. He was soaked with sweat. I felt his arm. Cold and clammy.

I didn't need a doctor to tell me Muley's ticker was struggling like an out-of-time motor.

Muley, the sturdy soul that he is, had managed a call to his wife, who's a nurse. She arrived maybe one minute behind me. She took one look and said, "Heart attack." I nodded.

Every minute counted now. I didn't think about that, but a nurse would say it again later, that we did the right thing when two of us—one at his shoulders and the other at his knees—picked him up and carried him to a waiting car.

His wife drove the streets of Macon like a Kamikaze pilot. I held Muley in place on the seat. His shallow breathing shouted an urgency that made me want to tell her to drive like a mad Kamikaze.

Then I could see the emergency room entrance. Hands helped me lift Muley out. And the hands wheeled him into a room.

Someone asked me his name.

"Muley," I said. "Everybody knows Muley, lady."

Then I sat in the L-shaped waiting room with Muley's wife. Her nurse friends gathered. Tears flowed.

I tried to feel good that Muley was in the Medical Center of Central Georgia. Wasn't it one of the best?

But nothing made me feel good.

Forty-five minutes after someone first told me Muley was sick, I saw him again. Some of his color had returned. He even told me he was feeling better.

But the damage has been done. His condition is still "serious." Doctors say his condition will have to stabilize before they can run tests to determine how much damage was done and what will have to be done.

I didn't sleep much Thursday night.

A few minutes after 8 a.m. Friday, I showed up at the Medical Center. Muley's wife was told that more then 50 calls had come in about my pal. Some callers just asked, "How's Muley?"

I wanted to see for myself, so I conned my way into the Intensive Coronary Care Unit. And I looked at him. Tubes ran in and out of his arms and nose.

He smiled up at me, and said the nurse standing beside me sure was pretty. At least there's nothing wrong with his vision.

He told me he's going to be all right. But I may not sleep again tonight, now that I know my hero isn't invincible.

Facing Surgery
Is Shakey Business

My pal Muley is going under the knife Monday for a triple-bypass operation, and I'm worried.

I sure don't want him to have a repeat of that May 12 heart attack. It scared the daylights out of me. But when they start messing with the heart, I get worried.

Surgeons are going to open up Muley's chest like a book and do a lot of things I don't understand. But as usual, my pal seems a little laidback.

I thought his medical trip was about over. I expected him back at work by now, sitting at the "liar's table" in the snack bar and telling stories.

But he sat there Thursday telling how medical experts flooded his veins with dye and then decided to do a little repair work.

Muley told me not to worry because *he* understands everything.

He understands, he says, because he was the resident pig doctor on the Turner County farm where he grew up. Let a pig come down with screwworms, and Muley was right there with the A-1 Screwworm Medicine.

In no time at all, the pig was as healthy as could be, and Muley was walking around smiling like a 'possum eating briars.

Yes, sir, Muley says he was just about as good a pig doctor as you could find anywhere. And that helps when they start explaining heart operations.

By now, he's heard detailed explanations about how they'll take arteries out of his leg and bypass three arteries that are blocked up and won't let enough blood reach his heart.

He says his arteries are so bad that he might not survive a Dolly Parton concert from a front-row seat.

One more thing. Muley has been on the operating table three times before, and he says one more trip isn't worrying him.

"Only thing I don't like about it is the cold," says Muley. "They let it get cold enough in there to freeze your fanny off."

As Muley sipped his coffee, I voiced my concern.

"What if they don't have enough spare parts?" I asked. "What if they get in there and find out they need something else?"

"Don't worry," he said. "These guys know what they're doing."

"Say, they're not going to use any parts from a pig like they did on that fellow from Atlanta, are they?"

"Naw, they'll get everything they need from my leg."

"Not if you need one of those valves. That would worry me. The fellow from Atlanta said he fell in love every time he passed a pig pen. I wouldn't want a pig's valve in me."

"You would if it meant living or dying."

"Well, maybe so . . . but I'm worried."

"OK, Ol' Boyd, what will it take to make you quit worrying about me?"

"Let me watch."

"Watch?"

"Sure. If I could stand close enough, I could make them stop if you say, 'Ouch.'"

"Listen, I'm not going to say *anything*. I'm just going to lie there asleep and let 'em do their thing."

"All the more reason I ought to be there."

"Would that make you feel better?"

"Sure would."

"OK, I'll talk to the doctors."

"Listen," I said. "You let those doctors know I'll be looking right over their shoulders. . . ."

"Sure."

"And if you oink when you wake up, tell them I want to know where they got the spare parts."

Meanwhile if you folks have any extra prayers, I'd be grateful if you'd say one for the best pig doctor I'll ever know.

After Surgery,
Muley Returns

Muley came to the office for a visit Monday. It's the first time he's been here since a quadruple-bypass operation on his ticker two weeks ago.

I handed him a letter from a lady in Vienna. Then I told him to sit down. He had some explaining to do. You see, I'd been trying to get him on the phone for several days.

"Boy, where the heck have you been?" I asked.

He deposited a sack of homegrown vegetables on my desk (he's a great backyard farmer), and he smiled.

"Out walking. The doctor told me to do lots of walking."

"Where do you walk? To Ashburn and back?"

"Just around the block."

"And how long does it take you to walk around the block?"

"About four hours."

"Four hours? It doesn't take *anyone* four hours to walk around a block."

"It takes me four hours. I have to stop and talk."

"Must be some pretty deep conversations."

"Well, sometimes they invite me to sit a spell. Lots of nice folks in my neighborhood, you know."

"What do you talk about for four hours?"

"Plenty. Mostly, we talk about being sick and having operations and things like that."

"Medical miracles."

"Well, not all of them. One is a real sad story. This fella—I guess he's younger than you—he has Lou Gehrig's disease. It's incurable."

"That's sad."

"But not all of them are like that. This one lady had her belly stapled together so she won't eat so much. That makes for some good conversation."

"I can imagine. So what else are you doing?"

"Well, tomorrow we're gonna start building my neighbor a swimming pool."

"Build a swimming pool? Have you lost your marbles?"

"Oh, I'm just gonna supervise."

"Supervise? Why do they need you to supervise?"

"Because they're having a hard time. They already cut down the only tree you could tie a rope on. . . ."

"Muley, nobody puts a rope in a tree over a swimming pool."

"I would. Down in Turner County, we had a rope tied to a tree limb over every swimming hole there ever was. But these folks already cut down the only tree. . . ."

"OK, OK. I'm glad it's gone. Tell me about the last couple of weeks. What's been the best part of it?"

"Being ALIVE!"

"Do you appreciate life more now?"

"Oh, I wouldn't say that. I never did have anything against living. I always liked it pretty much."

"But you really feel good now?"

"Yeah, and I feel humble."

"Humble?"

"Yeah, man. You think about this a minute. Here I am, sitting around talking and carrying on. And if it was just 10 or 15 years ago, I'd probably be sitting here waiting to die."

"Makes you feel humble?"

"Huuuuumble. And people make me feel good, too."

Muley was opening the letter from the lady in Vienna. He read it, and I could tell he liked what he was reading. He handed the letter to me. The neat handwriting said the lady in Vienna remembers him in her prayers.

Muley smiled. "That's what I mean about people."

"Listen, pal, call me once in a while so I can get a few words of wisdom on the hotter subjects, OK?"

"Sure . . . if I'm not out walking."

Things are just about back to normal around here, folks.

Hallelujah.

Muley and Mules

My pal Muley came strutting into my office last week with a copy of *Smithsonian* magazine. He was proud as a banty rooster when he pointed to a couple of mules on the cover.

Now Muley isn't a subscriber to that august publication. In fact, he was carrying November's issue. He said he knew it was a few months old, but a friend just gave it to him.

"I want to talk to you about this," he said. "You can get an education on mules from this article."

My pal and I often disagree about mules. I gave Muley his name because I said he's "as stubborn as a mule." Ever since then, he's defended mules as being smart, tough and—Lord forbid—even pretty.

Muley never tried to shake his nickname that I know about. He's just as liable to say, "Hi, I'm Muley," as he is to say his real name.

What bothers Muley—and is an ongoing point of discussion between us—is my evaluation of mules. He contends that horses are much more likely to balk than a mule. Not only that, he says, but mules are a whole lot smarter than horses.

"Now you take Doc," he said.

"Doc? That's a mule's name?"

"Sure. We always picked a short name for a mule—like Kate or Maude. They're easier to say. You don't want to say Christina Louise when you're mad."

"Well, how come mules usually have women's names. Aren't they sexless?"

"They're sterile and hybrid, not sexless. Hybrid. Remember that."

"OK."

"Do you know how we get mules?"

"Something about breeding a, uh, let's see, hmmmmm. . . ."

"You breed a jack to a mare."

"A jack. You mean, a, uh. . . ."

"Yeah, a male donkey."

"Oh."

"Anyhow, mules are smart. Doc was so smart that he could pick any type of latch we put on the door of the corn crib."

"That smart, huh?"

"Yes, and when you plowed with him, Doc never stepped over the traces like horses do."

"You never knew a clumsy mule?"

"Well, we had one named Ada."

"Ada?"

"Yes, my brother and I were riding the mules along a road one day, one in each rut. All of a sudden, he wasn't there. I looked around, and that darn mule had fallen into the ditch. I mean, its legs were sticking straight up in the air. Now if a mule can't get its feet on the ground, it can't get up. We had to get shovels and dig that mule a way out."

I asked if that didn't taint the perfect image of mules that Muley tries to paint. He said, "Never mind, just read the article."

He opened the magazine to a quote in large letters above the beginning: "Mules is born in a man; you ain't gonna get it out of him."

And right below that, it said, "Long bad-mouthed for cussedness, mules are in fact tough, smart, strong. . . ."

I could see I was in for an ear-bending.

He pointed to the third paragraph that started, "More intelligent than the horse and far tougher physically, the mule. . . ."

He even showed me the right wording about where they get mules. "A mule is the sterile hybrid offspring of a male donkey—or jackass—and a female horse." And mules were first "bred selectively for work in the cotton fields of Mississippi."

At least they didn't originate in Turner County. Muley never would've let me hear the last of that.

The article went on to say that the American Donkey and Mule Society has 2,000 members in 40 chapters. And people are collecting and showing them everywhere from the Missouri State Fair to Mule Day in Calvary, Ga.

"Y'see, mules *are* on the way back," he announced, closing up his prized magazine. "And I'll be waiting for that apology for all of the things you've said about mules."

Then he tucked the *Smithsonian* under his arm and strutted out.

Now don't y'all feel a whole lot smarter?

Muley
in the Mountains

Muley went to Hiawassee for the weekend. That wouldn't seem so important, except for two things.

First, Muley isn't a world traveler. The last time he ventured farther away than his boyhood home in Turner County, he wound up somewhere in Alabama. If he has to go farther than the corner store, his wife usually picks the roads.

Second, Muley had a time of it—from making reservations at Mull's Motel to listening to mountain music like he'd never heard before.

In case you've never been to Hiawassee, it's nestled in the North Georgia mountains no more than a hoot-and-holler from the North Carolina line.

Muley's adventure began with a long-distance phone call to the Hiawassee Fire Department to find out where he could stay. A fireman told him about Mull's Motel.

Aunt Emma answered at Mull's Motel and said he'd have to call back. Cordie Wood, the proprietor, was 'way out in the yard and couldn't come to the phone.

Since Aunt Emma seemed neighborly, there's no way Muley could feel put out by having to call back.

Second call: "Cordie Wood can't come to the phone because she's getting a permanent wave down at the beauty shop."

There's a big weekend coming up, Aunt Emma told Muley. Muley told her that's why he was calling.

Well, Muley still wasn't put out. Every woman has a God-given right to a permanent wave before a shindig.

Third call: "This is Cordie Wood, but some people just call me Cord Wood. What can I do for you?"

Perseverance pays off every time. Muley got his reservations for the big weekend. And he knew he'd even get to see Cordie Wood's permanent wave. He made a mental note to compliment her on it.

Muley said Mull's Motel is a nice place to stay. In fact, Muley's wife—being the South Georgia homebody that she is—even made up their bed after the first night there.

Aunt Emma came through bright and early with clean towels, and she thanked Muley's wife for the kind deed. Mountain folks appreciate visitors like that.

Muley said the two days of country and mountain music couldn't have been better.

"You shoulda seen this 5-year-old kid. They said he'd been singing since he was 20 months old." Muley thinks that's remarkable, since he told me he was 9 before he could wave bye-bye.

"That kid sang 'Elvira' and got everyone on their feet. He was great."

"Then came the mountain band. They sang music like you won't hear anywhere else. Even the same instruments other people play sounded different when they played.

"And one guy told some funny stories. He said they were going to sing a song they sung down in Gainesville that helped them build a brick building. He said every time someone threw a brick at them in Gainesville, they toted it home. And they finally got enough to build that building."

It was obvious that Muley grew pretty fond of mountain music and the unusual instruments those folks play. I told him I remembered a mountain man who made music with a moonshine jug.

"Weren't none of those there. They didn't allow none of that."

No, Muley, just the jug. . . .

"No moonshine jugs," Muley said emphatically.

Folks like Muley get a little huffy when you say anything that might reflect poorly on something as good as his weekend in Hiawassee. So I changed the subject.

How'd you get home, Muley?

"Well, we spent one night in Birmingham. . . ."

Now, don't laugh, folks. Don't you know Birmingham sits squarely between Hiawassee and Macon?

Porky Knew
About the Cold

Here it is, a cold Saturday morning with the weatherman talking about snow. Huddle up, lovers, and read about countrified weather predictions.

You probably watched the weather channel on TV or read the newspaper to find out when cold snaps are going to hit. My pal Muley used to watch the hogs.

Muley has a full litter of stories about hogs, but I didn't know a hog could forecast cold weather until he told me just this week. Muley said flat out, "Porky would have known it was going to get cold."

"Porky? Porky who?" I asked.

"Porky was a sow down on the farm when I was boy, and she would have known. Any pregnant sow would have known."

Let me refresh your memory about Muley and hogs. My pal grew up in Turner County, and by the time he was 12, he was the resident pig doctor on his daddy's farm just east of the Dakota community.

Muley administered doses of A-1 Screwworm Medicine and whatever else it took to keep a hog healthy until it was time for the trip to the sale barn. And knowing this, it isn't surprising that Muley's all-time favorite pet was a pig named Jake.

"It's amazing how good a pet a pig can be," he said.

I told him that a stick-fetching dog is more like my idea of a pet.

He said he understood. After all, Jake was pretty close to being a dog, "He took up with a dog. He followed that dog everywhere. Some folks thought Jake really believed he was a dog.

"He'd sleep on the porch with the dog, and he'd play around the yard with the dog. They'd chase one another, real playful-like."

But Muley says Jake just kept growing and growing, and he finally outgrew the games a dog and a pet pig can play.

Muley never revealed what happened to Jake.

Only thing I can figure is that Jake finally got fat enough that he brought a pretty fair price at the sale barn. Maybe that's why Muley doesn't talk about it. A boy can get pretty close to his pet.

Well, wipe the tears away and let's get back to Porky, the sow that could predict the weather.

"I grew up knowing that when the weather turned cold, you'd see hogs carrying straw. And Porky did that," Muley said.

"Carrying straw?" I asked.

"Yes, sir, they gather it up and build a bed with a wall around it to protect new litters of pigs against the wind and cold.

"Porky built the best bed I'd ever seen. I went looking for her one cold day just to make sure she was all right. I found her 'way out there in the wiregrass.

"I could see the wall of grass a long time before I could see her. It was this high," he said, holding a hand about three feet above the ground.

"She was having her first litter of pigs, and I guess she didn't know how high to build it to keep her little pigs' tails from freezing off."

"You don't mean that literally, Muley. It never really gets cold enough to freeze a pig's tail off, does it?"

"Sure, it does. The tails of the little ones, anyhow."

"I don't believe that."

Several other farm-wise people chimed in that Muley was preaching gospel.

"All right," I said. "So it gets that cold. What difference does it make? Do the little pigs die because their little tails freeze off?"

"No."

"Then, why worry about it?"

"Well, if their tails freeze off, there'll be a shortage of pigtails to eat that year."

"Aw, Muley, I don't eat pig tails."

"I know. You ain't much of a country boy."

But at least, now I can find out when the weather is going to turn cold . . . If I can find a pregnant sow. Here, piggy-piggy-piggy. . . .

HEROES
OF ALL AGES

*What makes a hero? Muscular men with superhu-
man strength . . . Maybe. But I'd also have to nominate a 7-year-old boy and a pregnant woman.*

Ricky Jackson: Crawford's Hero

ROBERTA—If there's one thing this world never gets enough of, it's heroes.

That's why we should never overlook one. And that's why I take great pride this morning in revealing the best-kept secret in Crawford County: the heroic deed of young Ricky Jackson.

It was Cub Scout awards night in Roberta. Ol' Boyd had finished a speech and was contentedly munching ice from a paper cup while Charles Cook and other scout leaders handed out pins for scouting accomplishments.

Then he called Ricky Jackson to the front of the room. The scout leader said the scouting medal for heroism was being awarded to Ricky for rescuing his little brother from almost certain drowning.

Really? I asked myself. How come no one ever told me about such a heroic deed by such a very young boy? Especially since Crawford County had been my beat for more than eight years.

Ricky took it in stride.

He smiled when they pinned the medal on his blue uniform. He walked quickly back to his seat as the audience stood and cheered. And he busied himself by looking at a hero's certificate while the noise died down.

When ceremonies ended, I cornered Ricky and his dad, Rick Jackson of Roberta. This is how it happened.

On Aug. 12, 1980, Ricky, then a lad of just 7, had slipped on his boots at his grandma's house next door to his father's house. He was going outside to do what all 7-year-olds do—play—when he suddenly was thrust into the role of rescuer.

Keeh, a 5-year-old sister, came running up from the pond shouting, "Come quick! Jeff fell in the pond. He's gonna drown." Jeff was the youngest of the Jackson children, a toddler of just 2.

Ricky's dad was at work. He told Keeh to "go get Momma." And he ran to the pond.

His little brother was making a futile effort to stay on top of water that reaches depths in that area of 17 feet. Clothes, boots and all, Ricky dived into the water and swam to Jeff.

Ricky stuck his head under the water and pushed up, balancing Jeff on his head and keeping him afloat. He repeated the process until his stepmother Angie reached the struggling youngsters.

Naturally, I had a few questions.

"Where did you learn to swim, Ricky?"

"My Uncle Scotty (Jackson) used to throw me in the water and make me swim."

"How old were you?"

"Oh, pretty young. About 3, I guess."

"I'll bet you're glad now that Uncle Scotty threw you in, huh?"

"Yes, sir. Sure am."

"What happened after you got Jeff out?"

"I couldn't sleep. I was afraid Jeff wouldn't be all right."

But Jeff was standing there Friday night, looking up at his "big" brother with the medal and obviously enjoying the attention.

"What are you going to do with the certificate?" I asked.

"Frame it and hang it over my dresser."

"And the medal?"

"Wear it. It's nice."

Just to make sure everything was all right Saturday morning, I called Ricky's grandmother, Mrs. Curtis Jackson in Roberta.

"He came in last night and said, 'Ya'll sure are going to be proud of me.' He showed us the medal, and we were very proud of him. We knew he had been recommended for it, but it had been so long that we had just about given up."

Mrs. Jackson said something else.

"Ricky couldn't wait to join the Cub Scouts. He had to be 8 or had to finish the second grade. He finished the second grade when he was 7, and joined right away."

Since scouts are taught to be helpful, brave and lots of other things, it isn't really surprising that Ricky Jackson answered the call, is it?

And even a little late, I thought you'd like to hear about a very young hero.

David Hammock's Scars of a Hero

HAWKINSVILLE—David Hammock is an educated man whose hands can perform all sorts of tasks from surveying to aerospace engineering.

But he failed in the simple task of trying to remove a young man from a burning car. The young man died, and, while some folks call him a hero, the Hawkinsville man lives with hands still scarred by his rescue effort.

And he lives with the memory.

David Hammock is an easy sort of guy to like. At 55, he's just about done it all. He reared five children and built a comfortable niche in life that includes good employment, a spacious home and a doting wife.

He wears a stylish Stetson over modish but disappearing gray hair. And he's gung-ho. I use gung-ho because David tried to join the Navy in 1941 when he was just 16. He wanted to join because other people were going halfway around the world to fight over a bombing that a kid in Rhine, Ga., could have known very little about.

The Navy wouldn't take him. So he waited a year and then volunteered.

For four years, David sailed virtually every part of the Pacific Ocean on a 108-foot, wooden-hull sub chaser. He never got a scratch from the war.

He came home, married former schoolmate Marinel Harrell and trekked off to the University of Michigan to earn an engineering degree. In the next 28 years, he worked in Ashland, Ky., Charleston, S.C., Washington, D.C., and Huntsville, Ala.

Five years ago, David and Marinel returned home to be near ailing parents and to give David a chance to be his own boss.

The Hammocks settled in Hawkinsville. David became Pulaski County's surveyor and carried on a private surveying business.

They bought a big house overlooking Abbeville Highway and settled down to the quiet life that was interrupted by little more than cries of grandchildren.

Maybe a guy like David Hammock ought to mellow a little with age. And maybe David did. But the gritty fibre of David Hammock never waned. Plenty of people found out about that last Oct. 27.

David came home that Monday afternoon and stopped in the kitchen to wash a day's work off his hands. He heard a muffled explosion. He looked out at the highway to see a pool of gasoline burning beside the road.

A car was burning, too. David Hammock ran to the scene.

A young man was screaming, "Ricky, get out of there." One passenger was still in the back seat of the two-door car.

David Hammock tried one door. It wouldn't open. He ran to the other side. That door was open, but the seat was afire. Despite the flames, he reached for the passenger, grabbing him under the armpits and pulling.

"It looked like such a simple thing," David said this week, "but he was unconscious and couldn't help."

David's son-in-law, Bobby Cleghorn, pulled the older man back from the raging flames. David yanked loose and plunged back into the fire again. The younger man pulled David back out a second time, telling him it was useless.

But David Hammock—his hide toughened by the war years and his life in the swamps and mountains—had to try one more time.

"It was a terrible, frustrating thing," he said.

Then Bobby pulled his father-in-law out the last time.

"I was convinced that last time that he (Richard Fowler, 18, of Pineview) was dead."

News reports of the accident didn't mention David's heroic efforts. But spectators remembered, and the story spread.

While others talked of his deeds, David gritted his teeth through painful treatments to remove the burned flesh from his hands. He said it was the most painful experience of his life—except watching that car burn.

Is David Hammock a hero even though he failed? Or is his act akin to the soldier who fell on the enemy grenade that didn't explode?

The Hawkinsville Fire Department honored him as a hero. So did the Hawkinsville Rotary Club.

On Wednesday, State Farm Insurance Co. will give him its "Good Neighbor Award."

Yeah, David, you're a good neighbor, all right. And a hero, too.

Rhonda Allen's Story for Baby

DANVILLE—We're always hearing about doctors who tell their pregnant patients to watch their weight and get plenty of exercise if they're going to bear healthy babies.

OK, but have you heard the story about the pregnant woman who rescued an elderly man from a house fire by physically dragging him to safety?

I'm not sure doctors want prospective mothers getting that kind of exercise, but Jim Fowler of Danville will tell you right quick that he's happy to have been pulled from a burning house by a pregnant woman named Rhonda Allen.

I know Rhonda, and although her heroics make me feel good, they don't particularly surprise me.

When I first met Rhonda, she was barely old enough to vote and was trying to break in as an electrician.

She's pure country, a tall woman with a ready smile, good upbringing and an infectious sense of humor. She's the type you'd want teaching your kids, living next door or waiting on you at the supermarket.

She was laid off the electrician's job some months ago. In recent weeks, she's been driving and helping Milton Brown, a blind piano tuner from Danville.

Rhonda Allen, 27, was leaving her home near Danville that Saturday morning a month ago to visit her mother in a Macon hospital. Rhonda had been battling a cold and she began coughing almost uncontrollably. She stopped the car.

That probably saved Jim Fowler's life.

As Rhonda got out of the car, a chill raced through her as she saw flames shooting out of a partially opened door of her neighbor's mobile home. Naturally, Rhonda, who is expecting in February, ran to the mobile home a short distance from the one she shares with her husband Tony.

If Rhonda felt a particular urgency in her flight, it's because Jim Fowler "is almost like a granddaddy to me." He's sometimes a dinner guest with the Allens. And he was a traveling companion for Rhonda when she played softball in leagues in Cochran and Jeffersonville.

"All I could think about was that he might already be dead. And it scared me," she recalled.

At the door with the flames shooting out, she saw a chair blazing ferociously just inside. She grabbed it and pulled it into the yard. She peered through the smoke. Jim Fowler sat in another chair.

"I hollered for him to come on and run. But he just stared at me, like he was in shock. He wouldn't respond. He just stared at me."

It was later determined that the elderly Fowler was in shock.

"I didn't know whether I could handle him or not," she recalled.

Desperately, Rhonda hailed a passing motorist, but it appeared that the motorist wouldn't be able to stop his car and run to the scene in time.

Then things "became a blur" to Rhonda as she plunged into the blinding cloud of smoke after her friend. She dragged him to safety.

"I don't know how I did it. I don't know how I handled him. I asked him later if his ears hurt. Maybe I dragged him out by them."

Then some semblance of order returned as others, including the motorist, arrived at the scene. Several people doused the fire, limiting damage to the living room. Others rushed Jim Fowler to a hospital where he was treated for shock.

Rhonda Allen went on to Macon to see her mother.

She acts like she didn't do anything particularly heroic that Saturday morning.

But now everyone knows better.

And I hope someone will clip this for the little Allen who will arrive in a couple of months. When the child gets old enough, he or she ought to read an account of how Momma got her exercise while she was pregnant.

Woody Dominy: Official Hero

Woody Dominy was a hero in World War II, a different kind of hero, but a hero nonetheless.

He never enlisted, never wore a uniform, never received the first instruction on how to fire any weapon.

Yet he fought more battles in two weeks than many soldiers, spent four years in prisoner-of-war camps and prisons, and prayed—like so many soldiers—that he would see his country again.

Last week—some 36 years after he came home to Georgia—the Navy sent him three medals, an honorable discharge and a nice letter.

James A. "Woody" Dominy, who grew up on a farm between Dexter and Rentz in Laurens County, didn't set out to be a hero.

He went to Wake Island in the South Pacific in July of 1941 as a truck driver with a civilian engineer group building an air and submarine base.

He was sleeping on that Sunday morning, Dec. 7, 1941, when a comrade shook him awake and said Pearl Harbor had been bombed.

Before he could get his shoes on, bombs began falling on Wake Island. "Everything broke loose, fuel tanks were exploding and machine gun bullets were hitting all over the place," he recalled.

Most of the 2,000 civilians on Wake weathered that first attack by shielding themselves with stacks of wall lockers and bunks.

When the planes went away, the commander of the small military garrison declared martial law and summarily inducted all of the civilians into military service.

For a week, bombs and artillery rounds rained down on the island. And the ensuing battle must have been one of the strangest of the war—untrained civilians without ample small arms and precious few artillery pieces—taking on a professional fighting force.

After a week of intense bombing, the Japanese attempted an invasion. But it was repulsed by the ragtag "draftees" with nothing more than outdated five-inch guns and four planes that survived the first bombing. The Americans sank several enemy boats and downed more than a dozen planes.

But the island group couldn't hold out. Surrender came on Dec. 23.

The first experience with their captors was the most frightening, Woody said. "They kept us lined up on the air field for two days and waited for word from Tokyo on whether they could take prisoners."

If the answer had been negative, Woody Dominy would have become a permanent war statistic. Instead, he became a POW, an alternative that meant being locked for weeks in the hold of a Japanese transport ship amid seasick comrades with only rice soup to eat.

He worried about the ship breaking apart in a typhoon and he worried about American torpedoes.

But he reached a concentration camp outside Shanghai, China. He spent three years there, picking up only occasional war reports on a primitive, homemade radio.

In the spring of 1945, he was moved to Omori Prison on an island in Tokyo Bay. More news filtered in through pilots who were shot down and captured while bombing the mainland.

And finally he saw the waves of American planes, the parachutes of red, white and blue bearing supplies and notes of encouragement. And he remembers the shouting, cheering and crying when American troops landed.

Then he came home.

Woody married a woman named Marie. They settled in Macon and brought two little Dominys into the world—Jimmy and Angelin.

The Dominys ran a neighborhood grocery for some years, and he operated a used car lot on Third Street during the 1950s. For the past 10 years, Woody sold cars at Riverside Ford. And he bridged the war years by selling a few American cars to friendly Japanese residents of Macon.

But Woody's 62 years are telling on him. He's nursing a weak heart and working only part time. But he dresses like a deacon and speaks in a soft voice. He kept his promise to God and became a really nice person.

But no one ever gave him a parade. No one pinned a medal on him. It wasn't until 1977 that a public law was passed that even recognized the Wake defenders as serving in the military.

Woody inquired about it, and last week, the medals arrived in the mail. He smiles a lot these days and shows his friends the rewards of those brutal, almost-forgotten years so long ago.

Come Veteran's Day on Wednesday, politicians and other leaders will say some nice things about the men who fought our wars. And this time, Woody, they're talking to you. Officially.

The Lavender Boys:
Brotherly Love

Poets, authors, philosophers—and even God—have lauded the kinship of brothers. But Daryl Lavender, a former Maconite now living in Gray, knows more about brotherhood than most people ever dare to guess.

Daryl, one of two sons of Herman and Alma Lavender, came into this world with an acute kidney malfunction. From the time he was born in 1947, his folks constantly administered medicine—from painful shots to pills so big he called them "horse capsules."

Without pills and shots, Daryl puffed up like a blowfish from liquid wastes his kidneys couldn't process.

The only thing he consumed that didn't back up into his system was watermelon juice. So his father, an employee of The Bibb Company in Macon, spent up to $35 each for watermelons imported in the off-season from Cuba to relieve his young son's suffering.

Sometimes, his fellow workers at Bibb passed the hat to help out. One woman anonymously donated $5 a week every week for several years.

Such charity can chip away at the pride of a working man like Herman Lavender, but an ailing son can make almost anyone accept a dole.

His medical odyssey took Daryl to Augusta and other places, but the answer was always the same—more pills, more shots, more treatments. Never a cure, just a means to live a little longer.

A brother was born when Daryl was 3. The Lavenders named him Andy. He grew up seeing his older brother punctured by needles or struggling to swallow those awful pills.

The Lavender brothers grew close in their growing-up years, a sickly Daryl and a husky, healthy Andy fishing together, running together. But the older brother lived 30 years to find out just how much Andy really cared.

Daryl's condition steadily deteriorated in his adult years. He was tired constantly. Some days, he managed no more than a couple of hours at the office of the Georgia Department of Revenue, his employer for the last nine years.

The medicine had less effect on him all the time. His kidneys shrunk even smaller and became ever more useless. And he knew he was facing the possibility of not being able to provide for his family—wife Karen and daughter Leslie, 3.

A little more than a year ago, Daryl described his condition as "getting worse all the time." He went to Dr. William H. Terry III of Macon.

The doctor inserted a tube into Daryl's wrist so he could be treated by a dialysis machine, but he never got around to the treatments.

The doctor told Daryl he had an alternative—a new kidney—if he could get one. The doctor was realistic enough with his patient to tell him that plenty of folks are standing in line to get a kidney. The wait might last longer than Daryl.

Enter Andy Lavender. He said he would give his brother a kidney.

But unanswered questions persisted. Among them: Would Andy's kidney be accepted by Daryl's body? Was Andy's kidney healthy enough? Would Andy survive without it?

The younger brother learned about pain. An incision was made in his stomach and a tube for dye was inserted into his kidney to aid in making much-needed, super-accurate X-rays.

And when all of the other questions were answered, one remained: Would a man really make such a sacrifice, even for his brother?

"He never hesitated, never gave any indication he wanted to do anything else," said a grateful Daryl.

Last Sept. 19,(1979), the operation was performed. The gritty Andy went home four days later and started building a new house.

Daryl followed three weeks later and helped his brother with the carpentry.

Now Daryl carries three kidneys—the two that function "at about 10 percent" and the good one from a brother. Andy gets by on just one. He seems none the worse for the donation.

Daryl told me this week—almost a year since the operation—that he never felt better, that he's down to just one kind of pill and that he's working every day.

And he wanted me to be sure to tell you one more thing: Andy is the hero of this story.

But I'll bet you already knew.

BEER JOINTS
AND BALLETS

Socializing in my part of Georgia means poolhalls, beer joints, country music, and, Lord knows, even ballet and high society. If you see only one side of this, maybe you'll enjoy reading about the other.

All About
the 'Cussing Can'

CORDELE—This is about drinking beer, cussing out loud and being a do-gooder, too.

You say they don't go together? They do if you have a "Cussing Can." Let me give you an example.

You've had a hard day, right? The car overheated on the interstate, and you had to hitch a ride to town to hire a mechanic who can't walk and chew gum at the same time.

You put up with that turkey for two hours and arrive late for an appointment in Cordele. Your prospective customer gave up on you and left for the day.

You wind up at the bar of the tap room of the Ramada Inn with a cool beer in front of you. But your weary hand accidentally hits the glass and you turn it over for everyone to see.

So you say something like, "Aw, $#&?¢%&$!&?#¢. I should have stayed in the #$%¢#&*¢&$ bed today. This has been the worst %&$&#$%!?#¢ day of my life."

Enter the "Cussing Can." It's held by a pleasant lady named Retha Holt. She's smiling at you from across the bar and saying, "That'll be 75 cents. We pay for that kind of language around here."

Now you're faced with either telling a lady to buzz off or coughing up 75 cents. Maybe being in a bad mood makes you say something like, "What the #$¢&#$¢*&% is this?" The lady ups the amount due to an even dollar.

But if you hang around, you can join a unique group of do-gooders.

It started with a birthday cake more than year ago. You know how it goes. Just as sure as you decide to have a beer bust for a birthday party, someone will order a birthday cake."

Any beer drinker knows that a slice of cake and a couple of beers can make your stomach feel like it made a trip down Thunder River. So the cake sits there until it's offered to some guy with half a dozen kids.

But not in this tap room. You give it to Libby Hightower. She's the chief of these do-gooders. She'll take it out to the local nursing home and put smiles on a bunch of faces.

In fact, she'll throw a full-scale bash for the oldsters by passing the hat to buy punch and getting tap room owner Floyd Keeney to donate plates, forks and other favors.

Folks at Crane Retirement Home will have a ball, and Libby will tell the do-gooders at the tap room about it.

Next time a cake shows up in the midst of beer glasses, you get Act II of "How to Make a Cake Disappear."

But why wait until another beer drinker gets a birthday cake, someone asked. And the "Cussing Can" idea was hatched.

Someone scrounged up an old coffee can and someone else produced a knife to cut a hole in the plastic lid. Twenty-five cents for bad words was the rule.

The "Cussing Can" did all right, especially with money-conscious Libby stretching the donations. But folks at the tap room saw more needs than 25-cent donations could fill.

Retha concedes that much more money comes from good hearts than bad mouths. "These are mostly young people—farmers and travelers—and they're good people."

And by the latest count, patrons of the tap room had collected and spent more than $500 in less than a year on the old folks at Crane. They even collected money one time to get a wheel-chair for an elderly man.

One salesman got caught saying the wrong word, and he was told the penalty. Instead of 25 cents, the salesman went to his car and came back with two dozen hair brushes for residents of the old folks' home.

And the "Cussing Can" keeps making the rounds.

Mathie Mims:
A Familiar Voice

I've heard the voice a thousand times before. I've heard it in churches, on the radio and echoing through my shower stall.

The voice never belonged to anyone in particular.

Parts of it remind me of several people.

Hank Williams used to sing, *Take these chains from my heart and set me free. . . .*

A woman who led songs in the church I attended as a kid sang, *Gimme that old-time religion, gimme that old-time religion. . . .*

And I sing in the shower, *My Uncle Bill has a still on the hill where he runs off a gallon or two. . . .*

The man playing the piano for me put all of those voices together—the perfect blend.

Mathie Mims is blind. And because he's blind, there have been times when music was his only entertainment, his only companion, his only expression of inner feelings.

I envy Mathie. He used to travel with bands and sing country songs all night long. There's no way music will ever mean as much to me as it does to this man, but I wanted to travel and sing when I was young. The dream faded after that woman in my church gave me the evil eye for getting an octave and a half above everyone else.

But Mathie never gets out of tune. A stroke six years ago didn't rob him of a good country voice and the ability to beat on the keys.

Mathie was born blind. He grew up in Colquitt County, and long before he entered the Georgia Academy for the Blind in Macon at age 16, he was playing an old-time pedal organ.

By the time he was 6, he would stand on the pedals of an old pumper organ and reach up to play the keys.

Without benefit of formal training, he learned music. Maybe that's where he gets his sound. Maybe it's something that can't be taught.

And when he went out in the world to earn his own way by folding card-board boxes or wrapping brooms, he always worked with a tune on his lips.

Music helped him earn his way, too. He never tried writing songs, but he played many instruments—organ, piano, harmonica, violin.

In the 1930s, his talent for so many instruments landed him on bands like Gene Mills and the Twilight Cowboys, Sleepy Cooey and the Rambling Hillbillies, and Ellis Wilson and the Dixieland Jubileers.

Mathie is almost 69 now and lives in retirement. He recently married Lillian Brown, a widow, and they live in a neat home on Jefferson Street on the north side of Fitzgerald. His home is easy to find because it's the only one with a handrail that leads from the front porch to the mailbox.

Several years ago, Mathie said he "got saved" and gave up playing any-thing but gospel songs. Most of his music is played at church gatherings, nursing homes and the like. He said that just before he and Lillian harmo-nized through several songs about Jesus and the hereafter.

I felt a little sad that he'd left behind so many of my favorites. But I didn't blame him. Those songs talk too much about drinking and cheating women, not exactly accepted subjects for church-going folks. . . .

Then his fingers began fluttering along the keys. "Let's see, now . . . Oh, yes. . . ." And he swung into a medley of old songs about pretty girls, cactus and sunsets.

He didn't sing anything about drinking or running around. And then he sang one more about Jesus just for good measure.

I told Mathie Mims that I would be back. His kind of music is good for the soul.

Ballet's
Not So Bad

PERRY—Y'all pat me on the back the next time you see me. I'm getting a little culture these days.

I went to the ballet on purpose Saturday night for the first time. That term "on purpose" is needed because I once stumbled into a ballet while looking for a Gene Autry movie in New York City in 1968.

My gosh, I thought, I've stumbled head-long into "bal-ette." You know, like "fil-ette" as in filet mignon.

Well, Marvalene and I decided to go on purpose because a friend, Valerie Jones, was dancing in Perry. In case you've never been to a ballet, let me tell you about this one.

But first, what do we wear to a ballet?

I knew it had to be something between what you'd wear to the governor's ball and overalls. So I chose a pin-striped suit, and Marvalene wore one of those spiffy suits that's perfect for Baptist weddings. I must say we looked pretty nice, my lady and me.

Second, our mode of travel.

The brand of wheels is important if you're going to mix in high society, and I didn't think it would be right and proper to drive up in front of this place in a '64 Plymouth missing two hubcaps. We took our customized van.

As it turned out, we might have overdressed a little. And we had to park 'way out in the dark where the van wasn't seen anyhow. But this is Perry and not New York City.

Now, about the performance of Rossini's *La Boutique Fantasque*. . . .

It started with some of what my old stepdaddy would have called "long-haired music." You know, lot of violins, playing in harmony and building to a peak that shook the innards of my hearing aid.

After about three minutes of music, the curtain opened. What I saw didn't surprise me. I know ballet dancers dress like . . . well, let's see. . . .

Those tights look sort of like my sweat pants—if my sweat pants suddenly shrunk about five sizes. I guess they look all right on younger men, but you couldn't pay me enough to get out in public in that get-up.

However, they look plenty good on female dancers. I noticed that right away.

One nice thing about the ballet is, no one talks.

You know how it is if you aim a spotlight at someone on a stage. They nearly always preach, make a speech or recite the Gettysburg Address.

In ballet, they dance. And even though there's nobody talking, you pick up on the story right away. I didn't need any help figuring out the plot of this one.

Two rich people bring their brattish kids to a toy store to pick out a Christmas present. Besides toys on every shelf, there are lots of dancing dolls. The boy-brat picks the lead male dancing doll, and the girl-brat picks the lead female dancing doll. These choices could break up a storybook romance.

But after maybe 15 dances filled with graceful acrobatics, the two lead dancers—still deeply in love, of course—get back together. And that's the way love stories are supposed to end, folks.

I liked the part when one dancer picked up the boy-brat and tossed him high and far off-stage.

When the curtain closed, Marvalene applauded like it was *her* daughter who'd been dancing up there.

And me? I clapped, too, but I was a little shocked to discover that ballet dancers really don't cheat when they dance on their tippy-toes. I thought maybe they were held up by puppet wires or something like that.

Then someone handed two bouquets of roses to the beaming Valerie, my ballet heroine.

Any ballet is supposed to end with ovations, of course. I'm glad this one did, too.

But when Marvalene asked Sunday if I'd like to see *The Nutcracker* in Macon, I declined.

Two "bal-ettes" in two days? Sorry, I said, but all I have left to wear is my overalls. . . .

Real
Poolrooms

CORDELE—It bothers me that the Real Poolroom is dying. You know the kind I mean—those scorned by housewives as dens of depravity, gathering places for loafers, havens for the shiftless.

What made the Real Poolroom so attractive to men? Well, it certainly wasn't women. I never saw a woman in a poolroom until after those "family entertainment centers" came along.

Those aren't Real Poolrooms, anyway. At least, not like the Cordele Recreation Center.

What makes this place different is chili dogs. The buns aren't different. The wieners aren't different. The splash of mustard and spoonful of onions aren't different. It's the chili.

The first time this poolroom ever saw me, I came to Cordele as a part-time sportswriter to report on a hot-rod quarterback named Mallon Faircloth and the football team at old Cordele High.

He's now a Superior Court judge, so you know how long it's been.

Two chili dogs and a Coke cost me 50 cents back then, and it was a meal. I never forgot the chili dogs.

Six or seven years ago, a trial brought me back to the Real Poolroom in Cordele. After a court session, former prosecutor D. E. Turk suggested chili dogs. Since then, I've been back several times.

Lately, I'm hearing disheartening reports about Real Poolrooms folding. That's why I went back this week to check on the place with the chili dogs.

Thank goodness, it hasn't changed.

Or has it?

Those really are women at the table in the corner, aren't they?

And aren't those video machines along the other wall?

But what about the chili dogs? A business lunch hadn't settled yet, but I had to know for sure, didn't I?

I ordered one. And a Coke, too, please.

Ummmmmm. Let the women shoot pool. Let the video machines beep and burp. Yes, sir, anything, but don't change the chili dogs.

A guy named Allen wiped his hands on an apron and watched me wolf down the chili dog and sip Coke from a bottle so cold that ice floated in it.

He assured me that chili was the same as 25 years ago. But the source of the recipe remains a mystery.

"I started working here 30 years ago as a cleanup boy, but I don't know where it came from. It's just something that was passed along through the years."

So I looked around at the pool hall, which replaced a drugstore in the B.B. Pound Building 33 years ago.

Sitting on a barstool, I reminisced about what made the Real Poolroom different from all the others. And just so you'd know, I compiled a list of qualifications for the Real Poolroom.

A Real Poolroom must have:

● A food that makes it different—hot dogs, sausages, chicken necks, something.

● Draft beer served in frosted mugs.

● A men's room that doesn't have a "Gentlemen" sign on the door.

● At least one guy in overalls shooting 8-Ball during lunch hour.

● Chairs high enough that you can see the tables without getting up.

● A sign that says "No Profanity." A sign saying "No Cussing" is even better.

● Some kind of partition between the pool tables and any video machines on the premises.

● Wooden cigarette bins behind the counter, rather than a cigarette machine.

The Cordele Recreation Center has all these things. If your favorite poolroom has five of these eight characteristics, it qualifies as a Real Poolroom.

So, rack 'em up.

Movin' in
High Society

ATLANTA—Just being in this metropolis is enough to tarnish a country boy's image. And eating here can reveal how uptown you are—or aren't.

Marvalene and I showed up at the Colony Square Hotel for a bash called the Georgia Music Hall of Fame Awards Dinner Saturday night.

First, we socialized for an hour. And, folks, you wouldn't believe the company Ol' Boyd was keeping.

Lt. Gov. Zell Miller was there, standing right beside me like an ordinary guy. House Speaker Tom Murphy showed up, too.

Brenda Lee was there. She smiled and shook my hand. I smiled and shook. She's one of my favorite all-time singers. I had a crush on her eons ago when she was singing on Tennessee Ernie Ford's show.

Gregg Allman was there. But I never had a crush on him despite my weakness for long-haired blondes.

Some of my friends were there—Richard and Sheila Greene and Tom and Linda Faulk of Macon. And include Ben and Vivian Jones in this group. Ben plays Cooter on "Dukes of Hazzard," but I like to think he's just plain Ben when he's not on my TV screen.

I didn't know it was truly a formal dinner until I sat down at the table and found myself looking at three knives, four forks and two spoons. I looked at Marvalene's setting to make sure they had enough of the same pattern to go around.

You'll have to excuse my ignorance, but my idea of a formal occasion is a watermelon seed spitting contest where they won't let you participate if you chew tobacco.

Marvalene knew I was in trouble, but she didn't know what to say.

Oh, well, the lieutenant governor was sitting at the next table. Surely I could find out something by watching which eating utensil he used first.

But that didn't work. He just talked. You know how politicians are.

Brenda Lee was sitting at a nearby table. I tried to see what she was eating with, but it's hard to see that far by candle light. Besides, she's married to this gorilla of a guy, and I didn't want him to think I was ogling his wife.

I sought help from my friends. I asked Tom Faulk if he knew which utensil we were supposed to use first. He said, "Sure, start at the top."

I asked him where he learned that. He said, "Twiggs County charm school."

Tom grew up in Twiggs County, all right, but he was putting me on. There really isn't a charm school in Twiggs County. Is there?

Anyhow, the top utensil was a spoon. And that stuff in the tall wine glass—shrimp cocktail, someone said—looked like it ought to be dipped with a fork. So I used a fork. I missed charm school.

Next, we dug into salad plates. I complicated the order of eating utensils even further by inadvertently using the butter fork to eat salad. And that waiter had his nerve. He took the butter fork away just as I was getting used to the little booger.

One sure way to tell when you're at a high-class bash: Ice cream is served before the main dish. They call it sherbet, and they say it's supposed to clean your palate—whatever that is.

Before I finished eating, the entertainment started.

While Freddy Weller, Ben Jones and Sammy Johns sang, I polished off the last of my main course.

While Gregg Allman and his mom were accepting a posthumous award for Duane Allman, I was using my next-to-last fork to eat pineapple-on-the-half-shell.

And when Brenda Lee was inducted into the Hall of Fame, I stood up and cheered like everyone else. She cried, and so did a lot of other people.

But Brenda Lee put a lot of tears in the eyes of young romantics with songs like "I'm Sorry" and "All Alone Am I." Maybe we finally got even.

When it was over, Marvalene asked what I thought about hobnobbing in high society. I told her maybe we'd go back sometime. Just to get our palate cleaned, of course.

TELLING IT
LIKE IT IS

Telling it like it is never makes everyone happy. But I like to think that it will make people speak out. And speaking out makes us better people to build better communities. Lord knows, that's hokey . . . but it's true.

Sharing
the Anger

There's an angry mood in my town. I can see why. I'm more than a little angry myself.

Once more, the issue of driving under the influence is making people's blood boil.

Maybe alcohol wasn't the only factor in the death of 4-year-old Charlie Dewayne Sinclair on Wednesday. Maybe we have to place part of the blame on carelessness. Maybe stupidity, too.

But the facts are very plain. Little Charlie died when a car smashed him from a curb of Norris Avenue in East Macon and dragged him down the street. The man police say was driving the death car was charged first with driving under the influence of alcohol and, a day later, with vehicular homicide.

Early Thursday, my phone started ringing. I wish the driver could have answered those calls.

"It's a #¢%&*# shame, that's what it is," said the first caller, who didn't give a name.

I didn't disagree with him. I just listened. "And did you read the story next to the one about the killing of a kid?"

It was 8:10 a.m. I barely had my eyes open. No, I hadn't read the other story.

"It's about Mike Jolly, the football player. His bond was $50,000 for possession of cocaine. The guy who (allegedly) hit the kid walked out on a bond of $1,485." And he swore again.

I waited.

"What's wrong with the #%$?!&#$*&% system?"

I have no idea why I tried to defend the bond system, but I said, "Bond is usually set at some figure just high enough to make sure the defendant shows up for trial."

He jumped on me like a dog on a bone.

After another U.S. Navy term for "dadgummit," he said, "Brother, if I'd been drunk and killed a kid with a car in Georgia, I'd post the $1,485, sell everything I own at one-tenth of what it's worth and haul my (expletive) to Mexico."

Anger never left his voice.

The next caller was a woman. She was crying.

"I lost a child to a drunken driver," she said, "And I'm going to call that mother and tell her what I wish I'd done, how I wish I'd sat through every minute of every part of the driver's hearing and trials."

She paused and I heard her sob again. "That driver served 90 days for killing my child. I'll never forgive the courts for that."

I didn't say anything, I couldn't think of anything to say. She hung up.

Others called. Charles Thompson said he sells insurance in that area, including Norris Street. He, too, is angry. And he also noted the difference in bond for the arrested driver and a man charged with cocaine possession.

By the time I went home Thursday night, I'd heard the bond thing aired a dozen times—at lunch, in the building, on the street, on the radio.

First thing Friday morning, the phone rang. It was the guy with the expressive vocabulary. I knew it was him when he said, "%$&*¢#?$¢. . . ."

I waited for him to get it out of his system.

"Did you read the paper this morning?"

I had him this time, "Yes."

"Did you see where they charged the guy with vehicular homicide?"

"Yes."

"Did you see what the bond is?"

"Yes. Just over $5,000, wasn't it?"

"Well, it's getting better, isn't it?" No one could miss the sarcasm in his voice.

"How's that?"

"You'd only have to be charged with killing 10 little kids to have to post the same bond as someone caught with cocaine."

"Well, now. . . ."

"Hey, are you going to try to defend this wimpy justice system again?"

"I don't know that I can."

"Which is exactly my point, brother, exactly my point."

Worrying About a Fallen Star

Mr. Claudell Washington
Star Baseball Player
c/o The Atlanta Braves
Atlanta, Ga.

Dear Mr. Washington:

I want you to notice the address at the top of this letter. Please read that second line again.

Maybe you weren't on the All-Star Team, and maybe you don't make the money Dale Murphy does. But I put the line in for a reason. You see, at our house, you really are a star.

To help you understand, let me tell you a little about my son, Joe. He's $12^1/_2$, going on 18.

I gave him his first baseball glove when he was 4. That was about a year after I gave him his first golf club. I'd hoped he would like golf best, but the kid went bananas over baseball.

But that's all right. When I was his age, baseball and the St. Louis Cardinals were a religion in Oklahoma. And I really believed that if I died, I'd go to Stan Musial's house.

Stan the Man. My hero.

Just before Joe turned 8, he played his first game of organized baseball.

I nearly busted my galluses when he socked the first home run ever hit in the new league in our end of town. The mayor—who'd thrown out the first ball just minutes earlier—autographed the ball and gave it to him. We took it home and put it in the china cabinet. It's there now.

I'm proud of Joe because he wants to be a good athlete, to grow up strong and healthy. Coaches had to jerk a knot in his shirttail once in a while, but baseball has been good for my kid, Mr. Washington.

In five years, he's done all right. He's played on two championship teams, and last spring he made the league's All-Star Team.

"Braves" was the name of the first team he ever played for. And about the time he started playing Little League baseball, we started making trips to Atlanta to see the "big Braves," as he called them.

Somewhere along the way, Joe started collecting baseball cards, too. He keeps them filed neatly in shoe boxes. Except for the stars.

He has a special box for them. You know, Dale Murphy, Reggie Jackson, Johnny Bench, Pete Rose, George Brett. He put their names on filing cards that stick up higher than the baseball cards. That way, he can find anyone he wants in a jiffy.

One day I noticed, Mr. Washington, that your name was among the stars. Joe said it was no mistake, that you're one of the best all-around players in the game. And I didn't argue.

Joe keeps close tabs on baseball. To do that, he reads the paper.

He reads the funnies pretty often. He even reads this column, if he finds it interesting. And he *always* reads the sports section, even in the off-season when Goose Gossage and Phil Niekro are moving around.

He reached for the paper Thursday morning. He never got to the sports section. His hero—you, Mr. Washington—was on the front page.

The headline read, "Claudell Washington reportedly treated for drug use."

My son flung the paper away and said in disgust, "Good Lord, even Claudell is in it."

He'd read about the others—Maury Wills, Pascual Perez, the football players. But they didn't bother him like you did. They weren't among the stars in the special box.

But I took up for you, I told him that at least you'd gotten help, that you weren't hauled in like a common criminal like some of the others.

Maybe in the spring—when flowers bloom and baseball returns—maybe then, everything will be all right.

By then my son will be a little older, and maybe he'll understand a little more about fallen stars.

Yes, sir, you're helping my son grow up, Mr. Washington. But this isn't the kind of help I need.

Ol' Boyd in Macon

No Jobs
for Quitters

One of my favorite places to visit is the office of Carl Peaster, principal of Macon County High in Montezuma.

The conversation doesn't always get so heavy, but on this occasion, I told him about not being able to find a job for a young man with no job training and no high school diploma.

You might think that's not so unusual, but I gave the job-seeker the best want ad in the world right here in this column. And when that didn't work, I went looking. I talked to people who employ maybe 11,000 people. I came up empty.

After I told Carl about this, he bared his soul on the subject. He said he is troubled by young people not taking school work seriously.

And he said intelligence isn't the problem. Motivation is.

His figures might embarrass some folks, but any student who finds a shoe that fits is welcome to wear it.

Carl said 18 percent of his seniors are flunking at least one subject. In the lower grades, the percentage is higher. And don't think his school is an exception. It's more the rule.

That's why Carl asked me to relate my job-hunting effort to his students. He said it might motivate them.

I scrounged up some figures of my own, and one morning, I strolled out in front of 540 students to tell them about looking for "The American Dream: A Job With Dignity." Here's some of what I said.

More than half of all high school students who fail to graduate with their class never will graduate from high school—not in a subsequent year, not by G.E.D., not *ever*.

And I told them that no one is looking for high school dropouts.

They're not needed to dig ditches, because machines do that now.

They're not needed as delivery boys because most businesses don't deliver anymore.

They're not needed in the armed services because high school grads are taking virtually every job.

They're not needed even to mow lawns. Many people have riding lawn mowers now and do their own.

I took the newspaper along and read some of the want ads.

Nurses? Yes.

Accountants? For sure.

Computer workers? Absolutely.

Electronics technicians? Certainly.

Mechanics? Always.

But nowhere could I find a want ad for dropouts, flunkees or quitters. Businesses and industries are looking for the trained, the skilled and the ambitious.

To let them know there's good money out there, I read the salaries.

Nurse: $16,000 to $22,000 a year.

Accountant: $20,000 to start.

Computer programmer: $13,500.

Electronics technician: $14,500.

Mechanic: $13,000.

I told them this country can never produce enough technological things—computers, airplanes and electric generators—to supply the demand. But we ought to be doing it.

Then I offered my solution to the nation's unemployment problem: Get everyone to move up one notch. Get every person to try a little harder, learn a little more, be better than they are. Most of us can do it without growing an ulcer.

That would allow unemployable people—if they will stay in school and get even a minimal education—to get the jobs they can't seem to find.

And you guys at Buzzard's Roost . . . well, you'll have to excuse me, but I told them what a sorry life yours is—how you freeze in winter and suffocate in summer just to make a few bucks.

If they quit school, I told them I'd see them at Buzzard's Roost. Or in the unemployment line. Or the welfare line. Or the county jail.

My job takes me to those places.

The people who really need to read this won't. Some can't. So I'll have to depend on others to try to sway some minds about quitting school.

And we really ought to do that. Every chance we get.

The Game
Is Revenge

When a Kamakazi in a pickup drove into the lobby of a Marine head-quarters building and killed 147 of our men, what did you feel?

Shock?

Revulsion?

Anger?

The need to retaliate?

I did. It happened in just that order.

At first, I thought those in the newsroom were kidding the old man who wore the Marine uniform for 20 years.

But it was tragically true. More than 120 Marines killed, early reports said.

Hey, those are my guys. You underhanded monkeys couldn't kill that many Marines in a month of Sundays in stand-up, hand-to-hand fighting.

One hundred and forty-seven dead, the later reports said. That struck a cord. I used to march 140 Marines in parades. With what happened in Beirut, not one soul in a company of Marines would have survived. My God, what a loss!

Unbelievable shock.

Then revulsion.

Dying never comes at an opportune time. You never really mean it when you say, "I could have absolutely died when. . . ."

But good Marines killed in the early morning hours by a pickup-driving suicide case? Smothered and smashed in the collapse of a four-story building?

While I'm feeling sick about this, I want to ask a few questions for 147 men who aren't here to ask.

● How did someone smuggle 2,000 pounds of dynamite through all of those checkpoints in Beirut?

● How did an everyday old pickup make it that far into the highly protected route into Lebanon's largest airport?

- How did a mere pickup manage to smash its way through gates, blockades and sandbags to reach the headquarters building?
- Why were Marines put up in a four-story building like that? Weren't they considered to be in a war zone?
- Has anybody been listening to the Joint Chiefs of Staff who wanted to move the headquarters back to the ships?
- Who's in charge there?

Anger? Retaliation?

Brother, you came to the right place this time. Somebody needs to pay a price. And I mean, a very high price.

But who?

The Shiite sect? Some reports say they were trying to help dig out our killed and wounded.

Moslems in general? They're enemies of the present regime in Lebanon, but did they do it? Probably not, reports say.

Someone mentioned Iran. It would be easy to hold them responsible after the time we had a few years ago with the nutty segment of that society. But what would you suggest? Pattern-bombing a few square miles of its capital? No, not that either.

Maybe the big-wigs in Washington ought to listen to a pal of mine. I won't name him, but he thinks there are better ways of dealing with terrorism than peace-keeping forces hung out in the wind like sitting ducks.

My pal says we ought to fight fire with fire, and he'd use "hit men" to do it. You know, mercenaries.

He says that hit men could wipe out the leadership in terrorist groups in a matter of weeks. And the leaderless mob wouldn't know where to plant its next bomb.

The price would be right. You could put a $1 million bounty on every baddie in the Middle East and still not spend as much as you would on one aircraft carrier.

And with this plan, we definitely wouldn't be planning at least 147 funerals in this country right now.

Some folks would say that Ol' Boyd isn't much better than the Kamakazi driver for repeating a proposal like that. But when I get this mad, I'll settle for almost any means of getting even.

And right now, revenge is the name of the game.

MARINES AND AMERICA

*"The Star Spangled Banner" and "The Marine Hymn"
still give me goosebumps every time I hear them.
When that doesn't happen anymore, y'all say a nice
prayer and lower my coffin gently.*

Remembering 25 Years Ago

If those guys at the baseball field hadn't asked me, maybe I never would have thought about 25 years ago.

But they wanted to know if Jack Webb exaggerated his role in that old film about Marines, "The DI."

Maybe you remember that scene where one of Webb's recruits slapped a sand flea while on night stalking maneuvers. Webb told them to find the sand flea "so we can give it a decent funeral."

Those celluloid Marines, frustrated by the search, concocted a plan to kill another and present it to the DI. But Webb asked, "Is that one male or female?" Of course, any answer given was wrong, and the search resumed.

My experiences a quarter of a century ago topped any of that stuff. On May 14, 1954, I started finding out what it was all about. I awakened that morning in Marine boot camp with a human lion roaring in my ear, "Get up, get up, get up. Off your bleep and on your feet: out of the shade and into the heat. Move, people."

I knew it wasn't Mom calling me for breakfast.

Staring out the window, I could see it was still pitch black.

But I got off my bleep and tried to do what the drill instructors wanted. A wise fellow who had been through it said to me, "Just stay in line and do what they tell you."

It wasn't that simple.

Lines formed alphabetically, and a little fat guy named Brown always wound up right behind me. On that first day, the DI noticed our Mutt-and-Jeff appearance.

The DI walked up to Brown and said, "Boy, I'm gonna trim that fat little bleep of yours right down to the size of . . . say, lad, what's your name?" he asked, looking my 132 pounds over.

I stuttered a little and then, with my best smile, said, "Bill." I wanted to be as friendly as Gomer Pyle later was with his DI. I'm sure my DI wanted to kill me, but he settled for simple assault.

Two quick blows to my midsection left me gasping for air, and, before he hit me a third time, I struck back in the only way I could—I threw up. He was lucky to get out of the way.

He followed me all the way into the barracks. "Stop that bleepin' puking, you hear. And when you're asked, you tell me, 'Sir, my name is Private Boyd.' You ever use that bleepin' first name of yours again and I'll. . . ." Lord, I was sick. But once we had that straightened out, I was ready for action.

But my platoon wasn't. We were awful.

You see, every Marine wants to be in the "honor platoon." Being number one is all that counts right then. But we were so bad the DI said that, on a scale of 1 to 10, we tilted the bleepin' thing in the other direction.

That's why we wound up sweeping the parade field. Ever seen the parade field at the base in San Diego? It's nine-tenths of a mile long and four-tenths of a mile wide.

We couldn't see why it needed sweeping. Any dirt on the asphalt surface was hidden in the cracks.

That's when we got out the toothbrushes. Seventy-five Marine recruits on their hands and knees with toothbrushes. We were pure speed and efficiency.

One of the guys tried to start a small rebellion by "accidentally" breaking his toothbrush. The DI told him he could do it with his breath. "Just keep blowing that bleeping dirt out of the cracks, and don't disturb the men with the brooms."

By 11 p.m., the DI decided to call it a night. At 4:30 a.m. we were back on our feet. As we gathered outside the barracks, we could see the pile of dirt. They'd need a dumptruck to haul it away.

Something turned us around. In the middle of the night, 75 toothbrush-wielding Marines got it together. We clicked, like two feet following one brain instead of the other way around.

We made honor platoon.

But I had a grudge to settle. I owed a DI something.

There's always a beer party after graduation ceremonies, and the DI was coming. My 132 pounds was 184, and I was just meaner'n hell. Bring 'im out here. Yeah.

The DI finally walked in . . . and everyone cheered. I did, too. I was still part of the team. That other thing could wait.

I even shook his hand.

That's a lot of memories from 25 years ago just because some baseball coaches asked me about being a Marine.

How Tough Is Tough?

With the stuff hitting the fan in Lebanon, the Marines are on the move again. It always happens this way.

Every time things get jittery, you see Marines—many of them not dry behind the ears yet—marching in ranks, boarding helicopters or catching 40 winks on the end of a seabag.

Anyone who played that game for 20 years remembers those other crises—Vietnam, Cuba, another time in Lebanon. And an old Marine who can't get his ammo belt around him anymore has to wonder whether this new generation—the one dealing with Iran, Libya and Lebanon again—is as tough as the old one.

I wonder if the "new" Marines can march 20 miles under a full pack, eat a platter of sukiyaki and then drink a case of green beer without falling asleep.

Yeah, I wonder if they're tough.

So I visited Maj. Sam Brinkley on a Monday morning.

"Are the Marines still as tough as ever?" I asked.

The major fixed me with a steady gaze and used the latest Marine term to describe today's Marines: "As tough as a woodpecker's lips."

Sounds tough enough, especially coming from an authority on the Marine Corps. Sam Brinkley has done just about everything a Marine officer can do in $11\frac{1}{2}$ years. He has been:

- A platoon leader in Vietnam.
- A rifle company commander at Camp Lejeune.
- Assistant director of drill instructor school at Parris Island.
- The man in charge of Marine recruiting in Georgia and South Carolina for the past year.

And along the way, he was once selected as the top company-grade officer in the entire Marine Corps.

The major talked enthusiastically about these "new" Marines. He said only the smarter, stronger men and women make it. And those who take drugs and most high school dropouts are prime candidates for civilian life. Some of his facts are interesting.

For instance, 87 percent of today's recruits are high school graduates. That compares with about 45 percent when I retired in 1973.

If a non-grad wants to stick around the Marine Corps, he'd better get a GED before it's time to re-enlist.

Boot camp now runs 11 weeks, up from 10 weeks when I enlisted in 1954 and far ahead of the eight weeks during the Vietnam War.

Physical training is tougher than it ever has been. But the physical quality of today's recruits is better, too.

Forty percent of those who enlisted as recently as 1980 would be turned away now just on academic standards.

Marine officials make regular medical checks to catch drug users. And the rule? One offense and you're out.

"The American people should have no lack of confidence in the young Marines in uniform today," Brinkley said.

Still, I wanted to know whether the Marines who might be sent into Beirut were as tough as some of my compadres who once went to airborne training at an Army base. (That one made *The New York Times*.)

An Army officer briefed the Marines on an operation. He told the Marines they would jump from 800 feet, regroup on the ground and march north.

One Marine raised his head and asked whether the altitude could be lowered to maybe 500 feet. The Army officer explained if the plane flew that low, there wouldn't be enough time for the parachutes to open . . . to which the surprised Marine replied, "Oh, you mean we'll be wearing parachutes."

That's when Sam Brinkley started talking about a woodpecker's lips.

Play it again, Sam. . . .

From the halls of Montezuma
To the shores of Tripoli. . . .

Left, Right,
Left, Right. . . .

A yellow bird with a yellow bill
Landed on my window sill.
I coaxed it in with a piece of bread
And then I stomped on his little head.
                                          —Military Cadence Song

Right away, I can see the ladies flinching at the thought of a big soldier stomping a little bird's head. It really sounds a bit cruel.

But when you're getting ready for war, ladies, cruelty runs in your blood and your songs.

On the other hand, most men will smile and remember lines of cadence songs they sang at Parris Island and Fort Bragg and Great Lakes.

The songs were simple and unsophisticated. No musical genius ever produced one. It took sweat and blood and the profanity of men going to war to produce these classics.

I'm sure no chaplain ever approved of them. And take my word for it, most of the lines of military cadence songs never will be printed in a family newspaper.

Some of the people who read this were never there, but unless you have been—huffing and puffing through a 20-mile hike with a drill sergeant breathing down your neck—you can't appreciate the pure unadulterated relief of singing a song like the one above.

Now I learn that Army Lt. Ralph W. Hamblin of Fort Benning is gathering these songs so they can be preserved in a book. He wants to document a passing part of American military culture.

I never thought a gung-ho old Marine would say it, but three cheers for this Army lieutenant.

An Associated Press report says many of the old cadence songs were considered "racist, sexist, sadistic or just plain vulgar." Lord knows, they were. Some described in detail the attributes of a girl from Kansas City and the sleeping habits of a girl from San Antonio.

However, there is little evidence that military brass ever tried to ban such songs through military directive. Maybe the brass is on the foot soldier's side this time.

Anyhow, Hamblin, the son of a career Army officer, has gathered about 100 songs by soliciting through military publications to veterans.

He says he learned in Officer Candidate School that many of the old chants were taboo. The rule of thumb at OCS was, "If you're marching or running past your mother, would she be offended?" he said. "We were left with a lot of 'left, right, left, right.' "

Hamblin said he got in trouble when he tried to sing a standard Airborne ditty: "C-130 going down the strip, Airborne daddy going on a little trip." Someone told him the word "daddy" was sexist.

His wife, who is entering medical school, didn't see anything wrong with the cadences.

"She thinks they're funny. . . . In a way, they're laughing at themselves, you know."

Undoubtedly, he didn't try some of those the Marines used to chant through Camp Pendleton while warming up for the war in Vietnam.

I tried a couple on Marvalene and she covered Joe's ears with her hands. But the wire story certainly stirred a lot of memories. . . .

He was born on Parris Island,
The land that God forgot.
The sand is 18 inches deep.
The sun is scorching hot.
He gets up in the morning
Before the rising sun.
He'll run a hundred miles or more
Before the day is done.
When he dies and goes to heaven,
St. Peter he will tell
Another Marine reporting, sir,
I've spent my time in hell.

And let's let the little bird get even before we finish:

A little bird flying overhead
Hit the man with the loaf of bread
Left, right, left, right. . . .

Working
Together

I get pretty tired of hearing how Americans are divided on this and at odds about that.

Take politics for instance. Republicans rule the U.S. Senate and Democrats rule the House of Representatives, and they can't get along. President Reagan is a conservative and House Speaker Tip O'Neill is a liberal, and they're always exchanging barbs.

How about North and South? Yankees talk funny and Southerners say sophisticated things like "Kiss my grits." A good old boy asks a Yankee, "Know what they call a pretty girl up North? A tourist. Hahahahaha." And the Yankee goes back home and tells the same story about pretty girls down South.

Husbands and wives. They're the worst. They often engage in an old American pastime—divorce. They fight and break up, and leave their children confused, frightened and alienated.

Thinking we got it together during the halftime show of the Super Bowl is pure cornball stuff. It's hokey to think about pride at a time like that, but I could feel mine grow a little.

A newspaper story said 112 million people would watch the Super Bowl. All of them wouldn't be Americans. That's why I'm glad we looked like we had it together.

I was watching the Super Bowl at Reese Towson's house. You remember Reese, the South Macon cowboy who now knows how to eat a waffle properly. We watched as the Miami Dolphins and the Washington Redskins battled to see which team members would get $36,000 each and which would get just $18,000 apiece.

And when halftime came, I started to head to the kitchen for coffee and some conversation with our football widows. After all, someone once said that if you really want to enjoy football, don't watch pregame shows, don't watch postgame shows, and don't watch halftime shows.

Naturally, I thought we'd be burdened with some mouthy commentator with a play-by-play dissection of the first half.

But TV cameras were busy with a halftime show called "Kaleido-SuperScope." And it really was super.

The sea of people in the stands—filmed by the Goodyear blimp above—turned red. I thought Reese's TV set was on the blink.

"Hey, Reese, the color on your TV just went wacko," I said.

Reese got up and adjusted the set. "Not much difference," I said.

"Best it'll do," he said.

The colors shifted again, this time to a purple and yellow pattern. That's when we realized the people in the stands were responsible for the change in colors.

Seems that those filing into the Rose Bowl Sunday were each given several cards of different colors. And they knew what to do with them. The 105,000 people in that huge bowl worked together like a well-rehearsed team.

And a couple of good old boys in Macon, Ga., ate it up.

"Great," said Reese.

"Fantastic," I agreed.

Several hundred people on the field were spinning and flipping colorful panels, but the people in the stands put the icing on KaleidoSuperScope.

As the announcer thanked 105,000 people for helping out, I thought about Americans who can't get it together—conservatives and liberals, Yankees and Southerners, husbands and wives. . . . Maybe so.

But I remembered other times in my adult life when we pulled together—the moon shot in 1969, the Iranian hostage ordeal in 1980, the Space Shuttle last year. . . .

We haven't forgotten how.

And I wished the Russians could have seen our Sunday show. I wanted those angry Iranians who constantly bad-mouth us to see it, too. And the East Germans, the North Vietnamese, the Chinese—everyone who ever chanted "Yankee Go Home." Yeah, I hoped some of them saw us.

Sunday afternoon, those 105,000 people in the Super Bowl, each with a handful of silly cards, made the ugly Americans look pretty darn good.

A Little Crazy
Is OK

Maybe it's good for our mental health to act a little crazy once in a while. But we pick the darnedest things to get crazy about.

Women seem most likely to do it, as far as I can tell. And before you start hollering male chauvinism, let me explain myself.

When I was a kid, women used to go bananas when certain items went on sale. I clearly remember hearing about how women would storm department stores in the industrial Northeast to buy nylon stockings.

I heard one story about a woman who was foolish enough to wear nylon stockings to such a sale. According to the story, this lady grabbed three pairs of stockings from the counter but lost the pair she wore before she could wiggle her way out of the mass of humanity.

Those sales never happened in quiet Oklahoma. Still, such stories made me dread the thought of ever having to live in a place like New York City or Chicago.

But I saw it happen at another place and another time.

When Elvis Presley got the world all shook up, young people went a little wacko. They'd pack as tight as sardines around a stage and scream their bloody heads off.

I went to a couple of his concerts. That's how I got hooked on "Hound Dog" and "Love Me Tender."

Young folks haven't changed a whole lot. Now they go wild when a guy named Billy Joel dances across the stage in his Nike shoes and jumps on top of a piano.

I watched one of his concerts on HBO one night and kept hoping he'd sing "Jailhouse Rock." But he didn't.

Watching the frenzied crowd on TV made me thank my lucky stars I live in quiet Macon, Ga.

Then a couple of things happened over the weekend that told me all of us have a little streak of craziness in us. Both of these happenings involved dolls.

A couple of visiting nieces think I've been living in a cave, but really, I'd never heard of a "Care Bear" until Thursday.

One of them pointed it out in a newspaper advertisement. Both of the nieces said they wanted to buy them before going back to Tennessee because the stores there always run out so quickly.

Then a neighbor said her daughter had gone that morning, and the "Care Bears" were sold out. You should have seen the long faces at my house.

But the quick sale of "Care Bears" at Aim was nothing compared to what happened Sunday at Zayre Stores in Macon when the "Cabbage Patch" dolls went on sale.

You probably read the stories about the crowd getting so wild that police were called in.

Good grief, that happened in Macon?

Sure did, my friend. And there's a reason.

Things haven't been good for us lately.

Little bush wars are threatening our peace of mind. We've been reading about a real wacko driving a bomb-laden truck into an American compound in Lebanon. We've worried about a little place called Grenada. The Russians walked out of the nuclear disarmament talks.

A lot of things are pressing down on our minds. Elvis isn't here to pack us around a stage anymore. Billy Joel is too busy for Macon and Greensboro and Tupelo. So we grasped at something else to help us through our little crazy spells.

"Care Bears."

"Cabbage Patch Kids."

We're willing to push and shove a little to put a smile on a daughter's or granddaughter's face. And do you know why? Those things are security blankets for kids. And kids prop up troubled adults.

Yeah, we're a little crazy. But we're crazy Americans. And that beats the heck out of being anything else and being completely sane.

Say, I wonder if Andropov ever heard of a "Care Bear". . . .

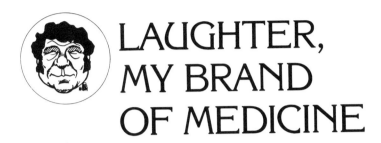

LAUGHTER, MY BRAND OF MEDICINE

Almost every day, a letter, a phone call, a conversation or a memory will tickle my funnybone. Since my first column appeared on Christmas Eve of 1977, we've shared a lot of laughs. Here are some of my favorites.

Miss Myrt Tells the Bare Facts

My friend Miss Myrt is much like my pal Muley in one respect. She knows enough true stories that she never needs to make up one. That's why I believe the one she related about a male stripper.

She told her story with lots of knee-slapping laughter, and maybe she embellished it a little. But I'll bet she didn't just make it up.

Perhaps you already know that male strippers perform in our town from time to time. I remember how huge throngs of women jammed the parking lot at one club several years ago when the first male strippers arrived.

And the tales I heard about how women acted!

One male waiter in the club said he absolutely would not serve drinks on nights the male strippers performed.

"Women get half-soused and they won't leave a man alone," he said.

I told him some men dreamed about having that "problem."

Well, I'm not going to mention any names regarding this latest story, but I'd bust if I didn't tell it.

The stripper who came to town a couple of weeks ago reportedly starts his act dressed in a policeman's uniform. I haven't seen him, so everything contained in this column today is pure hearsay.

Miss Myrt says she hasn't seen this stripper, either, but you know how women talk. Word about the performance—complete with daring descriptions, of course—raged through the grapevine like wildfire.

In Miss Myrt's own words, this stripper "must really turn the ladies on, 'cause I've heard all kind of tales about him." And you know women wouldn't make such a fuss over some wimp of a stripper.

Miss Myrt says women just naturally admire men in uniform, but maybe this stripper turned on the women *after* he shed the uniform.

At any rate, he had them screaming for more the night all of this allegedly happened.

Put all of these things together—women with drinks in hand, wild applause for a man who just stripped to the nitty-gritty, women nearest the stage stuffing money into the tiny garment that keeps him barely within the law. . . .

And into the midst of this madness walks a couple of local policemen who had arrived in the parking lot thinking a riot must be taking place inside, considering the screaming, screeching and yelping.

They walked into a, uh, tigeress' den.

The women in the back—those poor deprived souls craning their necks for a better look at what's happening on and around the stage—noticed that "reinforcements" had arrived.

They went absolutely bananas.

And that's when the "nightmare" supposedly started for the two policemen.

The women in the audience undoubtedly thought the two *real* policemen were part of the act, Miss Myrt says.

Hands went to grabbing. Others offered money to the two officers to "take it all off."

Miss Myrt quoted one of the policemen as saying he has an extremely jealous wife and that "she would divorce me in a minute if she'd seen what those ladies did."

But daring upholder of the law that he is, he broke loose, ran to his patrol car outside and radioed for backup units. Then he went back inside to extricate his partner from the clutches of women with stirred passions.

Miss Myrt was slapping her knee again as she told about the astonishment on the women's faces when they found out that those men dressed in police uniforms—except the lone performer, of course—were *real* police officers.

Now I hope all of you will believe this story. Everyone, that is, except any jealous wives of policemen who might ask too many questions about a man just doing his duty.

Remembering Hickeys

I hope you're not one of those folks who blush when I say hickey. Because today's subject is hickeys, necker knobs and drive-in movies.

Lord knows, it's been years since I've seen any of them.

First, let's talk about drive-in movies. If it weren't for drive-ins—and driving with one hand to get there—there surely would have been fewer necker knobs and hickeys.

Few adults pulled into drive-in movies in the early 1950s. And an angry adult could empty a drive-in in a matter of seconds.

For instance, I remember a man showing up one night with a shotgun. He was plainly silhouetted against the lights marking the entrance. Every teen there knew it was an angry daddy with murder on his mind.

I shoved Willie Lou aside, fired up my '41 Ford and headed for the exit. Two dozen cars clogged the exit lane. Lucky for me, it wasn't Willie Lou's daddy.

What allowed drivers to maneuver those old Fords and Chevys so expertly was a necker knob. At least, that's what we called it then in Oklahoma.

I've asked a dozen men who grew up in Georgia what they called it. They all said, "Well, uh, yeah, we had them. But that isn't what we called them, but uh, gee, I don't remember." One said it was called a "suicide knob."

The way they acted, you'd think they were 17 again and a mad daddy was heading their way with a shotgun. But I could tell they knew why the knobs were there.

A necker knob was a device that attached to the steering wheel to make it easier to handle a car before power steering came along.

We called it a necker knob because you could neck and pat your sweetie with one hand while you steered the car with the other.

Shifting gears was something else. But a guy named Butch once bragged he could steer with his chin, operate the floorboard gearshift on his

'39 Ford with his left hand and never take his right arm from around Willie Lou. Of course, that was before I started dating Willie Lou.

He was searching for second gear one night when the left tire hit a chuckhole. The necker knob came flying around and broke his jaw in three places. At school the next day, he said his jaw was broken in an awful fight with a bully from Tulsa.

When I started dating Willie Lou, she told me how Butch really broke his jaw. I learned to be careful about jilting girls who knew your secrets. Butch learned, too. I told his story all around town.

Now, about hickeys. Don't bother looking the word up in a dictionary. Daniel Webster must not have been a passionate soul. He calls it something besides a kiss mark. But you know what it is, right?

The first one I ever saw was on Willie Lou's neck. She had a Band-Aid over it. I pulled it off to look.

I asked her what it was. Her answer wasn't nearly as good as the one Mac Davis gave in a song the other night on TV. He said a squirrel fell out of a tree and bit him. Willie Lou didn't have that good of an explanation. I always thought Butch put the hickey on her.

Ask about hickeys and you'll get a lot of stuttering and stammering from your mate. Just ask him or her if they remember the last time they had a hickey. And then try to remember if you put it there.

I brought this subject up because I had a dream after Mac Davis sang about a hickey. I dreamed I got to heaven and found Willie Lou and Butch riding around in a '39 Ford with a floorboard shift and a necker knob. They were looking for the drive-in.

Willie Lou had a Band-Aid on her neck. I pulled it off. But before I could look under it, I woke up.

So I was sitting straight up in bed at 2 a.m., and Marvalene was asking what was wrong.

I told her I'd been dreaming about hickeys. It was too dark to see if she was blushing.

Grandma and the Flasher

She's really just a grandmother with Clairol covering the gray. But she knows how to handle a flasher.

You know what a flasher is. A person who exposes himself—or herself, I guess—to someone in public.

That's a pretty loose definition, but this is a pretty loose column subject.

Anyhow, Grandma was fishing from the dock near her lake home one day, just enjoying the warm sunshine. You know how that feels to old bones and rheumatism.

Old folks have enough problems just trying to catch their dinner on a hook without some smart aleck zipping past in a boat, stirring up the water and chasing the fish away.

But Grandma had other problems. This boat was pulling a splasher, a nut on water skis. After almost drowning our heroine in a sheet of water, he skimmed back out onto the lake.

Grandma was dripping wet and cussing mad. She shook her fist at him. He laughed.

Stomping up to her cottage, Grandma got out her binoculars and began scanning the lake for the offending boat. It took a while, but she spotted it, the skier now in the water.

As he crawled into the boat, Grandma hollered indignantly at the boat driver. The skier answered. She got flashed.

Just to make sure you understand, this guy pulled his bathing suit down and "mooned" Grandma with his bare behind.

Talk about a mad grandma. This one quickly scanned the boat for a number. She found it. Next step, the game warden.

The man in green quickly found the boat, hauled in the two young men and called Grandma. Lock 'em up, she said, for indecent exposure. The game warden kept the flasher for his parents. Seems he was only about 16.

His parents rescued the lad from the hoosegow, but Grandma wasn't through. Either a full apology is forthcoming or she presses charges, she said. The sham was over. She wasn't going to be a nice old girl. Not after being flashed, anyhow.

Wasn't long, she later recalled, until three people came walking up to her dock. One man, one woman, one teen-age boy. In her words, all three were "scrubbed church-going clean."

The older folks spoke. They were there to hear their son apologize for his short-lived career as a flasher.

But before the apology could be rendered that would hopefully end the sordid affair, Grandma spoke.

"From the actions of your son, I take it there is something special about his posterior. After all, he wanted to show it to me. He was quite far away, and I have no idea what might be so special about it."

The parents, noticeably squirming, said they already had made their son do such a thing in their den. They believed they had taught him a lesson.

"That's fine," Grandma said. "But now it's my turn. I'd like to see what's so special. After all, I couldn't see very well with all that water in my eyes."

Just when the nervous parents and teen-age son were about to have seizures, Grandma gave in. She'd settle for the apology, she told them.

She got it quickly and honestly, and one young flasher hurried from the dock where it all began.

To that I can add one thing. Hooray for Grandma.

Escaping from
the Ladies' Restroom

Everyone lives with dreads. A dread can be the worst thing that can happen to you short of getting a hangnail.

One of my dreads is winding up in a ladies' restroom. That's because it once happened to me.

Telling about it will take away one of Marvalene's favorite party stories, but I'd rather you heard it from me.

If you haven't been there, you can't appreciate the trauma that goes with sitting down in the wrong restroom. Imagine the embarrassment of getting caught in there and then getting exposed (no joke intended) as a peeping Tom.

You can make an excuse about being on vacation and how tough it is to find a strange restroom in a hurry, but who would listen to an excuse at a time like that?

In one careless moment, I rushed right in and sat down in the middle stall of the ladies' room.

In nothing flat, I had company. Voices. Women's voices!

I started to scream, "You women get out of here!" But before I could say anything, the thought hit me that maybe I made the mistake.

I stayed quiet. I didn't even breathe.

"Cynthia?"

"Uh-huh."

"Did you bring your purse?"

"Yes."

"Good. Can I borrow your lipstick?"

"Sure."

I sat staring at the floor, trying to figure a way out when it dawned on me that anyone glancing under the partition wouldn't think my shoes and trousers belonged to a woman.

I lifted my feet. And I sat there holding my breath and holding my feet off the floor.

Try that for one minute, and you'll understand why my fanny went numb in such a hurry.

Finally, Cynthia left her stall. I stole a deep breath when she flushed the john. Then I held my breath again while they dallied at the mirror.

When they left, I gasped for breath like a dying man. And I stood up and quickly arranged my clothes so I could make a dash for freedom from the ladies' room.

Forget the dash. More women arrived before I could open the door of my cramped little prison.

"I tell you, Ann, I didn't think Bob would ever stop. I may sit on the potty for an hour."

Lord forbid it, I thought.

Then I remembered my trousers and shoes again. Quickly, I *stood* on the john with one foot on either side of the seat, and I hunkered down so my head wouldn't show above the partition.

I waited. And waited. Would Ann stay an hour? Maybe.

I considered making a run for it right then, but Ann's friend left the stall on my right. I kept waiting.

A crisis. I absolutely had to clear my throat. But I knew a man clearing his throat wouldn't sound like a woman. Can a man clear his throat one octave higher than normal? I swallowed hard and tried to forget it.

Another urge. I needed to cough. Same problem. A man's cough just isn't like. . . .

They were leaving. Thank goodness. As the door closed, I stepped down. I wondered briefly if I could still walk. Feeling flowed back into my legs while I gave Ann and her friend a minute to get well away from the ladies' room.

Then I dashed for the door, whispering fervently, "Lord, don't let another woman come in here now."

The Lord kept them away.

One of the sweetest sights I ever saw was the empty hallway. But Marvalene was upset.

"Where have you been? I had an attendant look in the men's room, and he said you weren't even in there."

"I'll tell you about it in the car." I did, and that was a mistake. I've had to suffer through the retelling of that tale a dozen times since. Groan. . . .

Seeing the Sun Again

On the car radio that sunny Thursday, John Denver was singing about sunshine on his shoulder. He was hitting those high notes at the end as I parked in downtown Macon.

That's when I saw the man sitting alone on a bench near the new fountain in the Third Street park. He was soaking up the sunshine. In fact, he was looking almost straight up at the clear blue sky.

I passed close to him and I couldn't resist saying, "Sure is a pretty day, isn't it?"

"Beautiful, just beautiful," he said, lowering his gaze to me.

"Mind if I join you?"

"Sit right down. The seat and the sunshine belong to anybody that wants them."

"Can't beat that. Makes a man glad to be alive and free," I said, stretching a little and then settling onto the bench.

"Alive and free. Say, that's a right good line. And I'd have to add one more thing—warm."

"Warm?"

"Yes sir, I've been living 66 years, and I'm just now learning to like the sunshine."

"How come it took so long?"

"I was busy."

"Busy doing what?"

"Making a living. Seems I was always making a living. 'Way back when I was maybe 8 years old, I picked peaches down near the county line 'tween Perry and Marshallville. I was a little tyke, but I could pick peaches from the bottom limbs."

"But you didn't like it?"

"When peaches first come in, it's OK. It ain't too hot then. But by the time the last 'uns get ripe, the boss is hollering that they're gonna rot. By then, the sun is hot as blazes."

"Uh-huh. I never picked peaches, but I picked some beans and water-melons and okra when I was about that age. And it sure did get hot in Oklahoma."

He smiled. "I picked some vegetables down along the Florida line a few years, too. I remember it getting so hot that I'd lean my head just right so the sweat wouldn't get in my eyes. Yes, sir, I learned to hate that ol' summer sun."

"You always worked on a farm?"

"No, sir. I worked on the railroad here and there. Now, you talk about a hot sun! It don't get no hotter than on the railroad. No, sir, it don't."

"But you always worked in the sun?"

"Most always. Didn't have much education. And I had a wife and six young 'uns."

"And you raised them all?"

"Yes, sir, they're all grown now. Grown and gone. Wife's gone, too."

"Died?"

"No, sir, just up and left. Said she had enough of me. Just left. Didn't even give me a chance to talk about all that working in the hot sun."

"Women can be that way."

"I live alone now. Down there off Second Street. One of my boys lives with me when he ain't in jail. But mostly, he's in jail. Like right now."

"Really alone, huh?"

"Oh, I got a few friends . . . and today, I got the sun."

"Been a long winter, huh?"

"Yes, sir, and an awful winter."

He turned to wave to someone who passed along the sidewalks across the street.

"See? I got friends."

"Uh-huh. And the sunshine."

"You know how come I learned to love the sun?"

"How come?"

"Cause I almost died this winter. I was laying down there in that little ol' house, and I woke up one morning just after Christmas. I was hurting in my chest so bad I couldn't hardly stand it."

"Heart attack?"

"That's what the doctor said. But I didn't call no one that morning. I walked about 'leven blocks to the hospital. And they kept me for a while."

"That was a long walk. . . . "

"Yes, sir, that it was. I didn't know what was hurting me the most, the hurt inside or the cold outside. I thought I was going to freeze to death."

"But you didn't."

"No, sir. And I promised the good Lord that if I lived to see the warm sunshine again, I was going to stay out here all day long and tell him how glad I was he made that ol' sun I used to hate."

"That's why you're here?"

"Yes, sir, this is the first warm day since I got sick."

"Alive and free."

"Alive and free," he repeated.

I patted him on the shoulder and walked away. From across the street, I looked back. His gaze was cast toward the heavens again.

Alive and free. And warm.

Sunshine on my shoulder . . . always makes me high. . . .

Serving the Lord

If the good Lord stood right in front of me and said, "William J. Boyd, you *will* be a preacher, whether you *want* to or not," then I might consider it. After all, if he said my full name, I'd know he was serious.

But can you believe what the clergy have to put up with? Some examples:

First, there's the uppity woman who comes from unpolluted blueblood stock, and, by golly, she's not about to let the preacher forget it.

"My grandfather owned that table," she says icily. "It was made in Boston in 1688, and it was hand-rubbed by Alex Haley's great-grandfather. I *donated* it to the parsonage. And now *you*, a preacher who just came to *our* community two months ago, actually moved it out of the living room and into that *awful* basement."

Certainly the preacher moved it into that *awful* basement. When every blueblood in the county is trying to get a piece of furniture into the museum they call a parsonage, something has to go in the *awful* basement.

But believe me, furnishings are just the tip of the clergy's iceberg. Consider the preacher's social life.

The preacher is expected to attend virtually every party where booze isn't served. Just as sure as he or she plans a trip to Atlanta to see the Russians dance at the Fox Theater, he'll hear the voice of the guy who donated $12,000 to the church last year.

"My brother-in-law is visiting this weekend, and my wife says you *have* to come to dinner Friday night."

He doesn't say it, but that dinner fouled up his own plans to play poker Friday night, and personally, he couldn't care less about the preacher's.

Now tell me, dear reader, if you were a preacher, would you rather spend Friday night (1) at the Fox watching Russians tippy-toe across a stage, or (2) at a parishioner's house listening up close as some guy who brought halitosis all the way from Gary, Ind., tells you how steel is made?

And just as sure as you try to spend Saturday morning on the golf course with people you like, the woman who doesn't believe in spanking a child shows up with a child who could use a good spanking.

"I just don't know what to do with him," she wails. "He lies to me. He stole money from my purse to go to an R-rated movie. And this morning he shot the dog with his BB gun. Oh, please, help me settle this boy down."

Now, now, preacher. You must resist the urge to tell her to whale the daylights out of the unruly brat who's making faces at you.

Just scratch the golf game and get on with the counseling.

Then there's the married couple who have about as much business being married as Anita Bryant and the guy in the yellow tie. They're at a Mexican standoff in your living room smack dab in the middle of the Billy Graham Crusade on TV.

She's shouting that he's a drunk, and he's shouting that she's a nag. He threatens to "mash" her mouth, and she hauls out a 13-inch butcher knife she had tucked in her apron.

Don't just duck, preacher. And whatever you do, don't call the cops. The church couldn't stand that kind of publicity. Just trust the Lord and try to get that butcher knife away from the woman.

Then I read the newspaper Friday morning. Besides everything else, preachers are grossly underpaid.

Whether we want to admit it or not, being a preacher isn't just "answering the call of God" anymore. It means getting a very expensive education, serving an apprenticeship in many cases, and then waiting to get your own church so you can be underpaid.

And if you're lucky enough and stick with it long enough, you can make maybe $20,000 a year.

But for that amount, you also get a passel of bluebloods, status seekers, brats and prospective psychopaths. And you won't get to see many ballets or play much golf.

You've really got to love the Lord to live like that.

All My
Winning Losers

Six months ago, they wrote letters saying they wanted to lose weight. They faced public scrutinization and sometimes ridicule. But they were fat and they said so.

At first, the Lard Brigade stood 42 strong. Some quickly returned to strawberry shortcake and Big Macs. And we won't embarrass those drop-outs by publishing their names again.

When the time came this week for Ol' Boyd to pay up—a free meal for any man who lost 30 pounds or any woman who lost 20—fewer than a dozen showed. Several others deserved the meal, but couldn't make it to our dinner Wednesday night.

Here are the champs of the Lard Brigade—ladies first, of course:

MILDRED DYE of Gray lost $48^1/_2$ to a slim 134 pounds—"I love apple fritters, chocolate cake and fried chicken most. But I let a friend, Barbara Weathers, eat for me. I was asked a hundred times or more how I lost so much weight. When I said, 'Stop eating,' they said, 'Oh, yeah?' Now look at me."

JANET GUTHRIE of Macon lost 31 pounds to a most delightful (in the words of Ol' Boyd) 115 pounds—"I like chocolate, any way, any shape, any form. When the dieting got tough, I just mustered all of my will power and said no. I was doing exceptionally well until one night when my husband had a doughnut attack and went out to get a dozen doughnuts. I sat back and suffered. But I wouldn't trade my slim, trim 115 pounds for all of the doughnuts in the world."

DIANNA LUTZ of Warner Robins lost 22 pounds from a starting weight of 240—"Potatoes, bread and chocolate are my weaknesses. But I avoided potatoes and cut out bread. I was tempted often—like a co-worker who also is a Baptist preacher going out of his way to tell me when there was cake or doughnuts in the office. But I went on a high-protein, low-carbohydrate diet and took a walk instead of eating during my breaks and lunch hour at work. One problem was going TDY and facing all of the temptations that abound in that situation."

BETTY F. SMITH of Gray, down 20 pounds from 160 and aiming to lose 20 more—"I was hooked on pizza—among everything else that's edible. The night before starting (the diet), I ate up. So I started with no feelings of guilt. And nobody tempted me. They knew better! But in 25 years of marriage, my husband never knew my weight. Even when I stated that fact, you printed it anyway . . . and told the world . . . and my husband. But it's been fun."

And a couple of the men:

PETE NOVAK of Milledgeville, who shrunk from 284 1/2 to a mere 241 pounds—"I like pastas, ice cream, potatoes. I lost weight by sheer will power . . . plus being embarrassed helps. But it was a constant battle against the cakes and pies the lady of my house bakes. But my waistline is down from 50 inches to just 44."

LOUIS HUBBARD of Macon, down 35 pounds from 227—"I like fried foods any shape or size and ice cream anytime and anywhere. I'm the cook in our family, and many times I caught myself cooking the very things I shouldn't eat. So my wife planned the meals and did the cooking. When I started on my diet, I went strictly on juices. Everyone was sure I'd croak the first two weeks. But when I began losing and didn't die, I think they were encouraged, too. Now I eat one meal a day and sometimes two, but never an evening meal—except Bill Boyd's Lard Brigade's night out. Thanks for your encouragement."

And I'll bet you want to know about the others who made an accounting at the end of our six months.

Linda Faye Hunnicutt of Macon lost 23 pounds.

Roderick A. Herring of Macon lost 29 pounds.

Dinah Floyd of Cochran lost 30 pounds.

Bebe Chrismon of Macon lost 26 pounds.

Avoline Bloodworth of Oglethorpe lost 10 pounds.

Ray "Fatso" Lloyd (that rhymes with Boyd, he once said) of Warner Robins lost 36 pounds.

Stuart Stevens of Macon lost 19 pounds.

Larry Wisenbaker of Forsyth lost 15 pounds.

Larry E. Gilvin of Macon lost 30 pounds.

And Ol' Boyd? Just 14 pounds. One smart aleck said that's like dipping a cup of water from the ocean—no one will miss it. But I've changed directions with the lard, and you'll never know how good that feels unless you've tried it.

Sound Investment

Once in a great while, a story comes along I consider a classic. And only once in a coon's age will Ol'Boyd bother you with a dog story.

Now some folks say this story has been around since the University of Georgia was founded. Well, maybe. And then again, maybe not.

I heard it from a state trooper named Danny Ray of Perry. Here's the way he told it:

A south Georgia farmer wanted his only son to grow up to be a doctor or lawyer. And when the boy graduated from high school, dad took him to the University of Georgia. He enrolled the kid and paid for his books, tuition, room and board.

He gave the kid the old pickup. And then he showed his real love. He gave the kid $500 spending money. However, he explained that the money had to last all 10 weeks of the quarter.

No sooner was the old man out of sight than the kid's new-found friends initiated him into the night life around UGA. The kid had never seen so many beer joints and long-haired girls.

To say the least, he went a little wild. He spent money like it might catch fire at any minute. In two weeks he was broke.

He roomed with a third-year student who knew the ropes. "Don't use one of the old stories," said the friend. "Come up with a new one that your old man won't see right through. Parents have heard just about every excuse you can think of."

That's when junior remembered Old Blue, the dog—his dad's constant companion, a source of family pride because of his smarts, and a legend in South Georgia for tracking everything from fox to quail.

So the kid wrote:

Dear Dad:

I met the most interesting professor. He's an expert with animals, and when I told him about Old Blue, I could see his interest pick up. He said he'd like to try to teach Old Blue how to count, but it's expensive. He said it would cost $500.

I know how much you like Old Blue and thought you would want to know.

Two days later, Old Blue arrived special delivery in a cage accompanied by $500 and a note saying that "nothing is too good for Old Blue."

Of course, the kid tethered Old Blue on the clothesline behind the dorm, threw a couple of cans of Ken-L-Ration out there and headed out to Miller time.

Two weeks later, the kid was in financial straits again. But his innovativeness was just beginning to sprout. He fired off another letter:

Dear Dad:

Old Blue's progress is remarkable. The professor says he's the smartest dog he's ever seen. The professor says he thinks he can teach him to read, but it will cost $1,000. I know it's a lot of money, but I wanted you to know.

A couple of days later, the $1,000 arrived. Old Blue got another supply of dog food, and the kid hit the town for more beer and companionship.

This time the money lasted three weeks. Then the kid again took pen in hand.

Dear Dad:

Well, Old Blue has really done it. He's learned how to count. He's learned how to read. And now the professor says he can teach him to talk. But it will cost another $1,000. I know it's a lot of money, but I just wanted you to know.

Naturally, the old man sent another thousand. Old Blue got another supply of dog food and the kid returned to his wild and wooly ways.

That got him through the quarter, and he headed home for the break, Old Blue riding in the seat beside him. And he thought and thought. Finally, he performed a dastardly deed.

He pulled to the side of a country highway, got his pistol (all country boys own a pistol) and called Old Blue out of the truck. "Sorry, old fellow," he said and he put a bullet between Old Blue's eyes. He planted Old Blue in a cotton patch beside the highway and drove on home.

The old man met the kid at the front porch and welcomed him. Then he looked around and asked about Old Blue.

"Well, Dad, there's a sad story about Old Blue. Y'see, we were coming home, both of us better educated, of course. Old Blue was counting telephone poles. He must have counted a couple of thousand.

"Then he got bored and read the newspaper for a while, about the Middle East mess and all that.

"When he got bored with that, he started talking to me. And, Dad, the first words out of his mouth were, 'Sure will be good to see the old man . . . Say, I wonder if he's still messing around with that widow woman down on River Road. . . .'"

The old man grabbed his son's arm frantically and said, "Why, that big-mouth dog. I hope you shot the son-of-a-gun."

The kid said, "Sure did, Dad."

Hearing Aids: Getting Wired

When an audiologist hung a hearing aid on my right ear 18 years ago this month, he said I wouldn't wear it. He said very few people just 30 years old would wear one.

He blamed ego. He said it was especially true of young, single people who might be romancing the opposite sex. Since I was single and admired members of the opposite sex, I took the comment personal-like.

Well, I proved him wrong. Being able to carry on a normal conversation was more important than some stupid ego.

But the hearing aid posed a danger to something besides my ego. You haven't seen a man in trouble until a passionate young lady gets carried away in the vicinity of an ear with a hearing aid. One lick on a hearing aid, and the little gizmo shorts out and lights you up like a jukebox.

When Marvalene and I started getting serious, I made it clear that she ought to get serious only around my left ear, never the right.

She lit me up in public just once—in the back booth at Howard Johnson's many years ago. It was close to Christmas, and people there really got into the spirit. They sang two verses of "Hark, the Herald Angels Sing" before they realized I wasn't a Christmas tree.

For 18 years, I wore one of those hearing aids that rested behind my ear, a tiny tube carrying sound into the ear. I was glad I never had one with the big battery pack at the belt. People are always asking folks who wear those, "Do you have the Braves game? What's the score?"

Still, when I retired from the Marines, I let my hair grow long so few people even knew I wore a hearing aid. (That's my favorite excuse for long hair, anyhow.)

Actually, I was sort of glad to get my hearing aid away from mouthy Marines. One guy from Michigan used to torment me endlessly.

One day, he said in a voice just low enough that I couldn't catch every word, "Did you know a hearing loss is a sign of latent homosexuality?"

Naturally I said, "Huh?"

He left the scene of the crime before someone else repeated what he'd said. Last I heard, he was hiding out in upstate Michigan.

And when people asked me why a newspaper would hire a guy who wears a hearing aid, I'd tell them I hold an advantage over other reporters. By the time I write a story, the quotes have been said at least twice, usually loud enough for witnesses to hear. My stories are seldom challenged.

My old aid finally wore slap out after nine years. When I went for a new one, the audiologist almost flipped her lid when she looked at my record.

"Nine years, Mr. Boyd?" she asked. "Technology has passed you by."

She was right. I got rewired earlier this week. And in stereo, to boot.

Really, you wouldn't believe the difference. I now have *two* hearing aids, one fitted right into each ear. That's twice the risk with passionate ladies, but the sound is great.

I'm hearing things I never really heard before—and with remarkable clarity. Listen in with me:

- A commode flushing sounds a lot like Niagara Falls crashing down.
- When I brush my teeth, I notice that different size teeth and teeth with fillings make a different musical note. With a little practice, I think I can get the first verse of "Oh, My Darling, Clementine."
- Celery is the noisiest food to try to eat. Jelly beans are the slurpiest. And peanut butter sounds absolutely gross when you try to unstick it from the roof of your mouth.
- The passenger seat in my car rattles constantly, but then, Alabama never sounded better on my stereo.
- My "quiet" office now sounds like . . . well, like a dozen people beating on keyboards and a dozen others all talking at the same time.

I could go on and on with this list, but I really ought to print a warning before I finish.

I can now hear a mouse walk on cotton. And anyone making disparaging remarks about hearing losses may have to seek safety in the Michigan hills.

Now, I'll hear y'all talk to me in stereo.

Man Without a Coupon

Life is great in small towns. Folks there take care of one another and share things and get along. I'll give you an example.

Several weeks ago, my stomach growled so loud when I saw a fast-food restaurant that I had to stop.

The line was awful, but I couldn't stand another growl. I stood in line and took very shallow breaths so my stomach wouldn't growl. I'm not sure who told me that, but they said it would work.

One minute seemed like an eternity standing in the line. Finally, the guy in front of me—a sort of lumberjack in a hard hat—picked up the tray with two monstrous garbage-burgers, a pound of fries and a gallon of Coke, and went to a table.

The young lady at the cash register asked what I would have. I said, "Two cheeseburgers, a small order of french fries and a small Tab." I hoped no one mistook me for a lumberjack in a three-piece suit.

The clerk hit the total button and said, "Your coupon for the cheese-burgers, please."

"Uh, gee, I don't have a coupon."

"You don't have a coupon?" she asked incredulously. It seemed every-thing stopped while everyone gaped at the man without a coupon.

"Nope. No coupon."

"Everybody has a coupon," she said. The customer at the next cash reg-ister nodded agreement.

"I don't."

"Mister, don't you ever read the newspaper?" asked a voice behind me. Good Lord, what am I supposed to say to that?

"Listen, I just don't have a coupon," I told the clerk.

"You ought to take the paper. Our coupons are in the paper."

"Yes, ma'am," I said meekly to a woman half my age.

"Those coupons are good through this month and all of next month," she went on.

"Yes, ma'am," I muttered, suppressing an urge to tell her I couldn't care less.

"Well, that'll cost you another 38 cents without a coupon," she said.

"Yes, ma'am."

"And I'll have to get the cash register corrected. . . ."

The voice behind me spoke up again. "Vickie, I have an extra coupon. Let the man have his cheeseburgers."

The owner of the voice was another lumberjack in a hard hat. I was beginning to wonder if everyone in town had a hard hat. Did the clerk have a hard hat stashed under the counter?

"Naw, that's all right," I said. "I'll just pay the extra 38 cents."

"Really, mister, that ain't necessary. Looka here, I've got a dozen of 'em. I eat here 'most every day."

"That's very kind of you, but I'll pay the extra 38 cents."

He handed the coupon directly to the clerk and said, "Here, Vickie, this'll get the line a-moving."

I didn't argue anymore. I took my tray and looked for a table. The only vacant table was close to the cash registers. I wanted to get back in the corner so I wouldn't have to look at people who were looking at the guy who didn't carry coupons.

Then I heard the voice again. "Mind if I join you?" It was the lumberjack with the pocket full of coupons. I waved him to a seat and, really, we had some interesting conversation about small towns and coupons.

Then the lumberjack was nodding his head toward another city slicker in a three-piece suit. Vickie was saying again, "You don't have a coupon?"

The lumberjack pulled out still another coupon. "Want to help that feller?"

I took the coupons and walked to the counter. Vickie smiled. She knew where I was coming from. "No sense in having to correct the cash register," I said.

Yeah, life in a small town is really something.

Unwavering Resolve

Sermons at funerals always affect me the same way.

Some folks go to a funeral and cry. Nothing wrong with that. I've cried at a couple.

Some folks go to a funeral and stare at the flowers. They try to detach themselves so they won't cry in front of all those other people.

Not me. I listen to what the preacher has to say.

The sermon always seems important, even though it's never new. It hasn't changed much since I first heard it. Maybe it hasn't changed since the Bible was written.

The preacher always talks about how we have just so much time on this earth, how we ought not to worry about death, and how we ought to live a good life so that going to the hereafter will be easier.

The first time that sermon really sunk in, I was 17 and ready to graduate from high school. A friend had been killed in a hunting accident, and the preacher talked about how little time we have on earth.

I left the church that day with a deep resolve to get things done. My high school pal was gone, but, by golly, I was going on to college, get a degree and be *somebody*.

Three days later, I was wasting my time at a fishing hole, trying to catch a 25-pound catfish that was something of a legend in eastern Oklahoma. And three months into my freshman year, I quit college.

I never could explain what happened to that unwavering resolve.

By the time I was 21, a hitch in the Marines was about over. I was looking forward to civilian life and returning to college.

A friend died in a traffic accident outside Camp Pendleton, Calif. It was soul-shaking to me because I was talking to him just half an hour before the accident.

At a memorial service in the base chapel, a military chaplain talked about how our lives often hang by a single thread, and how we need to use our time here wisely.

The sermon sunk in once again. I said I would go back to college, get that degree and accomplish something important with my life. A few weeks later I re-enlisted in the Marines and stayed 20 years.

Unwavering resolve. Where did it go?

I heard that sermon again. One of Marvalene's cousins died in South Georgia. We drove there on a beautiful March weekend.

I sat in a little country church outside Blackshear and listened. The preacher, a clean-cut young man with an emphatic way of talking, said Cousin Miley had lived a Christian life and we all would do well to pattern our lives after her.

He said we ought to live right, be good examples and leave this earth without fear of the "next life." Maybe he wasn't talking about me, but I always take this sermon personally.

So I stared at the flowers and thought about my life. I'm a little old for college now, but I still have plenty of things to do.

Besides writing this column five days a week, I have a book that's started and another idea in the hangar. I want to write books because they might mean something after I've gone to my "next life."

But trying to work on a manuscript after writing columns all week is like a bus driver going for a Sunday drive. Still, I listened to the preacher and resolved to myself to make better use of the time remaining.

Coming home, my mind worked on something besides a manuscript. First, there was the three-hour drive home. It'll be 7:30 and I'll be worn out, I was thinking.

Monday morning, I'll be looking at five columns again. If I hustle, I can get it done, again.

With a little luck, I can get to Saturday morning with time to prop my feet up, drink an extra cup of coffee, maybe drop by the Little League field.

And my unwavering resolve? It's floating around here somewhere.

Burning Memories

She paused when I asked directions. That's when I noticed the bundles of letters in her small, time-worn hands.

"Lots of mail today?" I asked.

She smiled and said, "No, they're old—very old—love letters."

"Oh?"

"Yes, I'm going out to burn them."

"Really?"

"Yes. They're from Harry."

"Harry?"

"My husband . . . my late husband."

"Old love letters, huh?"

"Yes, very old, World War I."

"That's a long time ago."

"Yes, I was very young then. He was very handsome. We met on this street. He was attending Mercer. He quit school to join the Army."

"People don't quit college anymore to fight wars. They stay in college to keep from fighting wars."

"Yes, I know. But my Harry wasn't like that."

"He wanted to go?"

"Yes. He said all of his friends were already there. He was the youngest in his class, and most of the others had gone."

"And he just had to go?"

"Yes, he was only 18. He got on a train right down there, and he went away."

"And he wrote lots of letters?"

"Yes, so many of them. . . . "

"And now you're going to burn them?"

"Yes, they say too many things . . . too many intimate things."

"And that's bad."

"No, I didn't say that. I just wouldn't want anyone else to ever read them."

"Not anyone?"

"No, not even my own children."

"That intimate, huh?"

"Yes, I started reading one a little while ago. And I think I blushed."

"Harry wrote something like that?"

"Yes, he was very lonely over there. He told me everything about himself; how he felt about . . . everything."

"And it made you blush?"

"Well, yes. He just said some things about getting married . . . some very personal things. . . ."

"Harry said those things."

"Yes."

"Did Harry keep your letters?"

"No. My goodness, there was no way he could have carried all of those letters. I wrote every day."

"Every day?"

"Yes, Harry said my letters made the next day worth living while he was fighting through France."

"France. That's some place to be fighting a war."

"Yes, we went over there years later. Harry showed me some of the places where he fought. But it didn't look like there ever had been a war—unless you looked for bullet marks on the older houses and buildings."

She paused. "Are you married?"

"Yes."

"Did you ever go to war?"

"Vietnam."

"And did you write love letters to your wife?"

"I tried. I wasn't very good at it."

"Does she still have them?"

"I don't know."

"Did you ever write anything that would make her blush?"

"Yes . . . probably."

"If she still has them, what do you think she will do with them someday?"

"Probably burn them."

"Is that what you would want her to do?"

"I never thought about it before now."

"I didn't think about it until I read that first letter after all these years."

"And you're going to burn them?"

"Yes, I think it's time."

"And you think Harry would approve?"

"Yes . . . I think so. . . . "

She walked away, her steps short and slow. She stopped at a drum with rusty sides and black soot around the top from other fires.

The fire already was burning. She dropped the letters into it one by one, never once looking back at me.

I stood watching her. And I wondered if Marvalene would make a trip to a steel drum someday and burn a lot of old memories.